Environmental Issues

FRANCES MACKAY

TEACHER TIMESAVERS

Published by Scholastic Publications Ltd,
Villiers House,
Clarendon Avenue,
Leamington Spa,
Warwickshire CV32 5PR

© **1993 Scholastic Publications Ltd**

Author Frances Mackay
Editor Jo Saxelby-Jennings
Sub-editor Joanne Boden
Series designer Joy White
Designer Sue Limb
Illustrations Maggie Brand and Sue Hutchinson
Cover illustration Frances Lloyd
Cover photograph Martyn Chillmaid

Designed using Aldus Pagemaker
Processed by Pages Bureau, Leamington Spa
Artwork by Liz Preece, Castle Graphics, Kenilworth
Printed in England by Clays Ltd, St Ives plc

British Library Cataloguing-in-Publication Data
A catalogue record for this book is
available from the British Library.

ISBN 0-590-53065-8

Acknowledgement
The International Tidyman logo is reproduced on page 50 courtesy of the Tidy Britain Group.

Contents

Introduction

This book aims to provide a rich variety of activities on environmental themes. While some teachers may consider the topic to be more suitable for Key Stage 2 children, activities aimed at Key Stage 1 have also been included in order to cater for a wide range of ages and abilities.

The book is divided into the following sections: Materials and resources, People and their communities, Buildings and industry, Water, Weather and climate, and Plants and animals. Each section has cross-curricular activities which may include aspects of maths, science, English, geography, history and technology.

Each page comprises a photocopiable worksheet for the children to complete individually or in small groups. The sheets are ordered in each section by level of ability. Many of the activities include suggestions for class or small group discussion. Encourage the children to consider and value each others opinions. Where appropriate, references to National Curriculum attainment targets and levels have been incorporated in the Teachers' notes. For example, geography Attainment Target 3 Level 2 is expressed as Gg3/2.
❏ Denotes ideas for extension activities.

Materials and resources

What are these things made from? (Sc3/3; Gg5/1) Discuss, prior to the children completing this sheet, what some common items are made from; for example, jumper – wool – sheep.
❏ Make lists of school or household objects and the resources used to make them.
Natural resources (Sc3/3; Gg5/1) Discuss what 'natural resources' means, beginning with some common classroom objects; for example, desk – wood – trees.

Making use of rubbish (Gg5/2) This activity will require examples of each item on the sheet to be available so that the children can explore how the items could be reused.
'Our resources' writing paper (En3; Gg5) This page can be used at various levels and allows for a wide choice of subject matter. The attractive border also makes the sheet ideal for display.
Bookmark messages (Te2) The bookmarks illustrated should inspire the children to come up with their own ideas. Cover their finished designs with clear, self-adhesive plastic film to protect them.
Saving our resources (En2/2, 3/2) The picture and word clues make this activity suitable for very young and less-able children.
Using materials wisely (Gg5/2, 5/3) This activity should encourage the children to think carefully about the things they use each day and how they can reduce waste.
Possible ways of using materials wisely are given below:
• Buying wooden furniture: do buy furniture labelled 'wood from a sustainably managed forest'; don't buy tropical hardwoods.
• Using pens: do buy refillable ones; don't buy throw-away plastic pens.
• Using computer paper: do use the back of printouts for rough paper; don't print out more than you need.
• Empty cardboard boxes: do reuse them or recycle the cardboard; don't throw them away.
• Using envelopes: do reuse them whenever possible; don't throw them away.
• Buying eggs in cartons: do buy paper cartons and return them to the shop, if possible; don't buy plastic cartons.
• Buying paper: do buy recycled paper; don't buy more than you need.

• Buying take-aways: do make sure the packaging is minimal and can be recycled/reused; don't buy food in aluminium or plastic containers.
❏ Make a list of classroom or school materials used each day and how waste can be avoided or reduced.
Design a badge (Te2, 3, 4) Encourage the children to evaluate their finished badges and discuss which are the most effective.
Find the resources (En2/2, 2/3, 2/4) This activity aids familiarity with words associated with natural resources and encourages the use of dictionaries and reference books.
❏ The children could make up their own word searches.
How green is your school? (Ma5/2, 5/3) This survey will help to highlight environmental awareness in your school. It may also identify future environmental needs in the school.
❏ The children could design their own survey sheets, with questions relevant to their school.
My pledge to help protect the world (En3) This statement encourages children to think about their lifestyles and how they might improve them for the sake of the environment.
❏ The children could design a pledge to improve the school environment.
Saving energy in the home (Ma5/2, 5/3) This activity will make the children aware of the ways in which energy can be saved and may encourage them to take positive steps to reduce energy use in their homes.
❏ Ask the children to find out how much electricity can be saved by various energy-saving ideas, such as loft insulation.

What does it mean? (En2/3, 2/4) This sheet enables the children to become familiar with environmental terms and encourages the use of dictionaries and reference materials.
❏ Encourage the children to use the words and their meanings to construct a crossword.

Renewable and non-renewable resources (Gg5/5; Sc4/5) Much class discussion may be needed before the children attempt this activity. Some resources are classified as non-renewable because they take so long to re-form, for example fossil fuels such as coal and oil.

Make a word search (En2) This activity aids familiarity with resource words and also provides some problem-solving opportunities when the children are asked to design their own word searches.

Reusing rubbish (Gg5/2, 5/3) This activity is similar to 'Making use of rubbish' (page 15), but requires a higher reading ability to complete the sheet. It also encourages investigative work at school and home.
❏ Conduct a survey to discover which families from the class, or school, recycle their waste.

What are fossil fuels? (Ma3/4; Gg3/3) When using coordinates, emphasise that the positions are located by going along the base first (letters) and then up the columns (numbers).
❏ Challenge the children to make their own environmental words using coordinates.

Erosion (Gg 3/4) Preparation will be necessary for the children to complete this sheet; they will need to know what erosion is and how it occurs. If possible, visit local sites that demonstrate erosion and discuss which could be prevented.
• Hikers will wear away the plants and topsoil, nothing will grow there.
• The ice repeatedly melting and freezing will cause the stone to crack and crumble away.

• The river will wear away the banks and river-bed, carving out a deep gulley and may form ox-bow lakes after flooding.
❏ Discuss which types of erosion could be prevented.

Going shopping (Gg5/3, 5/4) A display of products from a supermarket or a visit to a store will enhance this activity. It will allow the children to read the information on labels and to see how things are packaged.
❏ An interview with a supermarket manager (or a letter to a manufacturer) could be arranged to discuss why certain products are sold as they are; for example, why is plastic used and not glass which can be recycled?

The world's resources: 1 (Gg5/2, 5/3; En2/4) Reference books will be needed for this activity.

The world's resources: 2 (Gg1/2) This activity encourages the use of an atlas and will provide information about where many of the world's resources come from.
❏ A map of British resources could be produced. This could be extended to finding out about resources imported and those exported.

Producing electricity (Sc4/3, 4/4; Gg5/5, 5/6; En2/4) This activity encourages research into energy production and the alternatives available.
❏ Discuss which types of electricity generation should be used in the future.

Saving fuel (Sc4/5; Gg1/4, 5/3, 5/4 and Ma1/4) This sheet provides a problem-solving situation. Let the children compare their results to find the best route.

People and their communities

Pollution words (En3/1, 3/2) Providing the alphabet will make this activity easier for some children.

❏ This activity could be extended by making an ABC of pollution words and presenting it as a book or wall display.

Air pollution (Gg5/2) This sheet could be used as the basis for small group discussion or as an individual task. A teacher or helper could act as scribe for younger or less-able children when compiling a list of ways to prevent air pollution.
❏ Let the children draw pictures showing where air pollution occurs in their school or neighbourhood.

Pollution I-spy (Sc1) This activity helps develop observation and recording skills. It could lead to much discussion about the causes and prevention of pollution.

'Pollution' writing paper (En3) This page allows the children to write down their own information/ ideas about pollution. The attractive border should encourage the display of work.

Consequences (En3; Gg5/2) This sheet encourages the children to predict what might happen if different types of pollution occur. It may promote discussions about how people are responsible for looking after their environment.

Noise pollution (Ma5/2, 5/3) The results of this survey could be presented as a graph.
❏ Ask the children which sounds annoy them most and why. Which sounds do they think are important (for example, ambulance or fire-engine sirens)?

Design a 'green' machine (Te2, 3, 4) A collection of pictures of machines may provide a stimulus for the children's own designs. This activity provides an opportunity for the children to design according to a set of needs. Encourage them to evaluate their designs on the basis of whether or not they have met these needs.

How people affect our environment (Gg5/2) This activity may be used in conjunction with the 'Consequences' sheet (page 40). It encourages the children to think about how one action can cause something else to occur.

Design a litter bin (Te2, 3, 4) This sheet provides the children with an opportunity to design according to a set of needs. Encourage them to evaluate their designs on the basis of whether they have met these needs.

Journey to school (Ma5/2, 5/3; Te2, 3) This activity encourages meaningful investigation into transport – it may even encourage children to find alternative means of getting to school without causing pollution!
❏ Let the children design posters or badges that will encourage others to walk or cycle to school.

Traffic survey: 1 (Ma5/2, 5/3) Make sure there is suitable supervision for this survey. In a busy area it may be best to share the types of vehicles among the children and collate the totals back at school. A graph of the results could be produced.

Traffic survey: 2 (Ma5/2, 5/3; En3) This sheet allows for an analysis of the data collected during 'Traffic survey: 1' (page 46). It may involve group or whole class discussion or research before the questions can be answered fully.

Litter survey (Ma5/2, 5/3; En3) The litter need not be touched, merely recorded. The results could be collated as a graph.
❏ If possible, issue the children with strong rubber gloves and plastic sacks so that they can collect the litter and dispose of it properly.

Taking positive action (En3/3) Class discussion about relevant issues may be necessary to stimulate ideas. Hopefully, the children will receive a positive response! Encourage them to use a desktop publishing program such as

Caxton Press: an introduction to desktop publishing (1989, Birmingham: Newman Software) or *PenDown* (1986, Cambridge: Logotron).

Signs of the times (Te2) A collection of objects with symbols on them will provide a stimulus for the children's own ideas. Ask them if they know the symbols for: recycled, ozone-friendly and poisonous/toxic. Encourage them to compare their finished designs to evaluate how successful they are in conveying the message.

Playground litter (Gg1/3; En1, 3; Ma5/3; Te2, 3) This activity could follow the 'Litter survey' (page 48) as it is an extension of the data collected. By mapping where most litter is found, litter bins can be placed more strategically.
❏ Suggest that the children design badges to encourage others not to drop litter.

Improving your school environment (En1, 3) It is by engaging in activities such as this that awareness is raised about how people can change their environment for the better.

Design a car park (Te2; Ma1, 2) This sheet provides opportunities for problem-solving and could be tackled as a group activity. You could enlarge the sheet to use toy cars.

Headline news (En3) This activity could be tackled at various levels. It may be a good idea to look at real newspaper articles first to discuss how they are written and how reporting differs from other types of writing.
❏ The finished article could form the basis of further work with the computer, using programs such as *Caxton Press* or *Front Page Extra* (1987, Birmingham: Newman Software).

Environmentally safer cars (En2, 3)
Across: 2 solar; 5 catalytic converter; 6 unleaded. *Down:* 1 journeys; 2 share; 3 fuels; 4 less.

❏ Encourage the children to make up their own puzzles.

Polluting our planet (En2, 3) Make available reference books for this sheet. Group discussions may help to stimulate ideas.

'Going green' (En2, 3) Reference books will be necessary for this activity.
❏ A survey could be conducted to see how many children use the 'green' ideas in their homes.
❏ Suggest that the children use these ideas to design 'green' badges or posters to inform others in school about environmental issues.

For or against (En1, 3) This activity could form the basis for a class debate on the issues which emerge. It may be necessary to provide reference materials so that other people's opinions on the matter can be considered.

Buildings and industry

Industry crossword (En2/2, 3/2) The picture and word clues make this activity suitable for very young and less-able children.

Good or bad? (En1) This activity could be approached at different levels. Older children could use the pictures to stimulate poster designs or as ideas to create their own information books.

An ABC of industrial needs (En2, 3) Provide reference books for this activity. The words could form a word bank for further writing on the topic or they could be made into a large wall display.

New shop (Te2, 4) Encourage the children to discuss each part of the building (the windows, door, roof, sign writing and so on) so that they blend in with/match the buildings around.
❏ Visit a shopping area near the school to look at building designs; do they blend in or could improvements be made?

A better place to be (Gg5/2, 5/3) This sheet is similar to 'Our street survey: 2' (page 65) but it is of an imaginary place and could form the basis of a 'practice' for the real-life survey.

Our street survey: 1 (Ma5/3) A separate sheet could be completed for each building or one sheet used for all the buildings. The results could be compiled as a graph.

Our street survey: 2 (Gg5/2, 5/3) If it is not possible to visit a site, photographs or magazine pictures could be used for this activity.

Supermarket terms (En2, 3) This activity will encourage the use of dictionaries and reference materials to help provide familiarity with the words used in the topic. Make a collection of supermarket items with suitable labels, such as ozone-friendly.

Clues about industry (En2, 3) This is a problem-solving activity. Practice as a whole class may be necessary before individuals tackle this task on their own.

A greener home (Gg5) Provide reference books and encourage a sharing of ideas.

Finding out about buildings (Gg5) This activity could be carried out together with the 'Our street survey' sheets (pages 64 and 65), allowing the children to choose one particular building to study in more detail.

Is it biodegradable? 1 and 2 (Sc1/2, 2/2) If no site is available at school, ask the children to bury the objects in their gardens at home. Encourage them to think of reasons why things will/will not rot away. Instead of using sheet 2, the children could devise their own recording sheet.

Streets of change (Hi1/2, 1/3, 3/2, 3/3; Gg5) If possible, find photographs of old and modern buildings near school so that the children can discuss the changes that have taken place.

Invite one or two of the children's grandparents in to talk about street-life in their young days.

Industry – past and present (Hi1/2, 1/3, 3/2, 3/3; Gg5) Reference books may be necessary for this activity. Encourage sharing of ideas.

Water and industry (Ma2/4)
❏ The children could contact local industries to find out how much water they use and what methods, if any, they use to minimise this amount.

How industry can affect the land (Gg5/4) If possible, visit a gravel pit site or quarry so that the children can have first-hand experience of a mining environment.

Become a town planner (Gg5/4) The children could attempt a plan of the classroom before moving on to this activity to provide familiarity with the task.
❏ A visit to the local town council planning office could provide further insight to this issue.

Interview a shopkeeper (En2, 3) Invite a shopkeeper to school or arrange a visit to your local shops.

A new factory (Gg5/4) Provide opportunities for the children to share their ideas in groups.

Industry – resources and waste (Gg5) Provide reference books for this activity.

Supermarket impact (Gg5; En1, 3) This activity could form the basis for a class debate on the issue. Encourage the children to try and understand the points of view from both sides.
❏ Suggest that the children write a letter to 'Mr Smith, Town planner' saying why the store should or should not be built.

Water

Polluting the sea (Gg5/2) This activity could be used as the basis for a small group discussion or as an individual task. For younger or less-able

children a teacher or helper could act as scribe when making the list.

Water – where do we find it? (En2/2, 3/2; Gg3/1, 3/2) The picture and word clues make this activity suitable for younger and less-able children.
❏ If possible, take the children to various sites where water is found. Discuss different forms of water such as rain, ice and snow.

Water – how do we use it? (En2/2, 3/3) This activity is also suitable for younger and less-able children.
❏ Can the children think of other uses of water and then paint pictures of them?

Water – how is it polluted? (En2/2, 3/3; Gg5/2; Sc2/3) The picture and word clues will help younger and less-able children. The activity should also encourage the use of dictionaries, if the meanings of some words are unfamiliar.

River pollution (Gg5/2) This activity could be used in conjunction with the 'Polluting the sea' worksheet (page 81). A teacher may need to act as scribe to answer the question about cleaning up the river. Encourage the children to work in groups to share their ideas.

Water – saving it or wasting it? (Gg5/2) Group discussion may be necessary before this sheet can be attempted.
❏ Invite the children to think of ways to save water at school.

The water cycle (Gg3/2, 3/3; Sc3/5) Whole class or group discussion may be necessary before completing this sheet.
❏ Encourage the children to think how the water can become polluted at each stage of the cycle and how such pollution could be prevented.

Design a poster (Te2, 3, 4) This activity can be attempted at various levels. Encourage the children to consider colour, lettering and the message they wish to convey and let them discuss how the poster might be improved.

Polluted water – a comic strip (En3) This comic strip format may encourage reluctant writers and can be attempted at various levels. The children will need to study the pictures and make inferences about the story. Ask them to share their stories – are the same conclusions drawn?

Water words (En2) This word search aids familiarity with water words and encourages the use of dictionaries and reference books.
❏ The children could devise their own word search puzzle.

Water poems (En3) It may help to make a few class or group shape poems to stimulate ideas before attempting this activity.

Match the meaning (En2) This sheet encourages dictionary use and will assist the children's understanding of the words they will encounter in this topic.

How clean is your pond or stream? (Sc1, 2/3; Gg5) Discuss and emphasise safe behaviour, including not leaning out over the water, wearing suitable footwear, not drinking the water and reminding the children to wash their hands after the visit. Also consider a 'Code of conduct' for visiting the site, for example, disturb as little as possible, leave no litter and so on.
❏ This activity may lead to a community improvement project cleaning up a local river or pond.

Continue the story (En3) This sheet can be attempted at various ability levels and will suit individual or group work. Encourage the children to share their stories to compare ideas.
❏ The stories could provide a basis for more work on pollution/conservation, for example, role-play.

The water game (En2) This game will remind the children of some of the causes of water pollution as well as reminding them of ideas for conservation and improvements. For this game, the children will need one die and a counter for each player.
❏ The children could design and make their own board game.

Obtaining water (En1, 2, 3; Gg5/4) This activity encourages deduction and idea sharing.
❏ Ask the children to find out which countries obtain their water in each of the three ways.

Using water at school (Ma1, 2, 5) This sheet should raise the children's awareness of how much water is used and wasted at school and may initiate measures to reduce the waste.

In order to work out how much water is used, allow the average number of times that the toilets are flushed and hand basins are filled to be three times each per child or adult per day (morning, lunch and afternoon). The amount of water used in the classroom sinks could be calculated on the basis of one classroom and then multiplied by the number of classes. To find out how much water is used in the kitchens, ask the school cook to keep a tally and then encourage the children to interview the cook in order to access this information.

Rivers of the United Kingdom (Gg1, 2) An atlas will be needed for this activity. The rivers marked are: 1 Spey; 2 Dee; 3 Tay; 4 Forth; 5 Clyde; 6 Tweed; 7 Tyne; 8 Wear; 9 Tees; 10 Ouse; 11 Mersey; 12 Trent; 13 Nene; 14 Great Ouse; 15 Severn; 16 Wye; 17 Thames; 18 Test; 19 Avon; 20 Exe; 21 Tamar; 22 Bann.
❏ The children could go on to find out where the sources of these rivers are located and how their water is used. Contact with your local river authority may provide information about water

usage and pollution levels in your locality.

How much water do you use? (Ma2, 5) Use the survey results in a computer program, such as *Grass: a data handling program* (1987, Birmingham: Newman Software), or produce a graph. Which household uses the most water and why? How could water be saved?

Uses of water (Gg2) Provide atlases for this activity. Group discussion will be very important to compare ideas about the consequences of each water use. Explain that the effects of some uses of water are not as straightforward as they might seem. For example, irrigation is essentially good, but can be harmful if there is insufficient drainage. The land in very dry regions usually contains alkaline salts which dissolve into the irrigation water and permeate the soil. If the drainage is inadequate, particularly in low-lying areas such as the Nile floodplain, then the salts are deposited and can poison the soil.

Who has clean water to drink? (Gg2) This sheet is designed to raise the children's awareness of the problems in some countries of obtaining fresh drinking water. Ask the children to suggest why most of the countries are in Africa and Asia. The countries marked are: 1 Paraguay; 2 Morocco; 3 Senegal; 4 Gambia; 5 Guinea Bissau; 6 Guinea; 7 Sierra Leone; 8 Liberia; 9 Ivory Coast; 10 Mali; 11 Burkina; 12 Togo; 13 Benin; 14 Nigeria; 15 Niger; 16 Chad; 17 Sudan; 18 Ethiopia; 19 Somalia; 20 Kenya; 21 Uganda; 22 Zaire; 23 Central African Republic; 24 Cameroon; 25 Equatorial Guinea; 26 Congo; 27 Angola; 28 Mozambique; 29 Madagascar; 30 Rwanda; 31 Burundi; 32 Oman; 33 Afghanistan; 34 Bangladesh; 35 Myanma (Burma); 36 Malaysia; 37 Indonesia; 38 Borneo; 39 Java; 40 Papua and New Guinea.

Weather and climate

Weather crossword (En2/2, 3/2) The picture and word clues make this puzzle suitable for younger and less-able children.

'Feeling under the weather?' (En1, 3) Group or class discussion may be needed before the children attempt this task individually. Encourage them to compare their feelings and the activities they like to do when particular weather conditions occur.

❏ These feelings and activities could be acted out in role-play sessions or pictures painted.

❏ Ask the children to imagine what it would be like to live in a place where the weather was always the same – how would this affect the way they felt and what they liked to do?

Protection from the weather: 1 and 2 (Te1, 2, 3, 4) The examples given in this activity should provide stimuli for the children to design their own clothing suitable for different kinds of weather.

❏ Additional tasks may include designing and making a stand for the model and/or designing houses, clothes or equipment suitable for different weather conditions or seasons.

A change of season (En2, 3; Gg3/2) Provide reference books and encourage the children to share their ideas in groups.

❏ This activity could be extended by discussing such issues as depletion of the ozone layer or the Greenhouse Effect. (For example, if the world's climate became warmer, how would this affect the seasons and our environment?)

Protection from ultraviolet radition (Te1, 2, 3 4) Prepare the children for this activity by discussing and investigating the properties of light. Also discuss why it is important to protect the skin to help prevent skin cancer. Provide examples of sunglasses, hats, gloves and footwear for the children to look at as stimuli for their ideas. Models could be made from clay, boxes, fabrics and so on.

❏ Have a fashion parade of the children's designs – entrance fees could be donated to an environmentally-aware cause.

Climate and buildings (Gg3, 4) This activity could be attempted without the children having any prior knowledge of the housing types in different countries because it encourages deduction from the pictures of the qualities necessary for each climatic type.

❏ Let the children draw pictures of their own homes and ask them to label all the features that protect their houses from the climate. Models of the houses could be made and scientific investigations carried out on them, such as investigating waterproofing and insulation properties, structural strength and so on.

Changes in the weather (En3) This activity encourages the children to project into the future; to predict what might happen to plants and animals in the environment. Provide opportunities for them to discuss what might happen if certain weather conditions continued for lengthy periods.

❏ Additionally, discuss what would happen if the wind did not stop blowing on a cornfield and/or it rained every day on a river.

What would happen if...? (En3) This activity encourages prediction and postulation. The sheet could form the basis for group or whole class discussions after completion. For example, if the sea level rose, cities situated on river banks such as London, would be flooded, forcing people to move to higher ground. Sea water would flow into freshwater supplies contaminating drinking water, farm land and animal habitats. Encourage the children to think of ways to prevent these things occurring.

The ozone layer (En2, 3) This activity encourages the use of reference books and will provide the children with background knowledge to complete other activities in this section, for example, 'Save our ozone layer' (page 112).

Save our ozone layer (Te2, 3, 4) Encourage the children to think about lettering, colours, the message they want to get across and so on.

❏ Study skills could be developed through finding out more about CFCs.

The Greenhouse Effect (En2/3) This is an exercise in comprehension skills and will provide the children with background knowledge of the Greenhouse Effect. The activity may also involve research skills to find out what various terms mean, for example CFCs, fossil fuels and gases.

Acid rain (En2/3) This sheet provides background information on acid rain and encourages the children to use reference materials to find out the answers to the questions.

Acid rain – a worldwide problem (Gg1, 2) This sheet could be used as a follow-up to 'Acid rain' (page 114) as it extends the children's knowledge of this problem and highlights affected cities around the world.

The cities affected are:

LA = Los Angeles; NY = New York; C = Chicago; S = Santiago; R = Rio de Janeiro; A = Accra; Lo = London; Li = Lisbon; M = Madrid; P = Paris; At = Athens; Co = Copenhagen; St = Stockholm; H = Helsinki; B = Baghdād; T = Tehrān; Bo = Bombay; D = Dhaka; HK = Hong Kong; Sh = Shanghai; Se = Seoul; Ma = Manila; Si = Singapore; J = Jakarta; Sy = Sydney.

What causes air pollution? (En1; Sc2/3; Gg5/2, 5/3) This activity is designed to support work already carried out on air pollution because knowledge is required of acid rain, the Greenhouse Effect and the ozone layer in order to complete the task.

❏ The children could draw pictures of other sources of these pollutants and add them to their groups.

Weather word search (En2, 3) This activity encourages the use of dictionaries and reference books and provides familiarity with weather words.

❏ Encourage the children to write their own word searches.

The world's climate (En2, 3) This puzzle is a cloze exercise to develop comprehension skills and aid familiarity with climate words.

Across: 1 CFCs; 3 global; 5 coal; 6 ozone; 7 methane; 9 oil; 10 energy; 11 catalytic; *Down:* 1 carbon dioxide; 2 smog; 3 greenhouse; 4 gases; 8 acid rain.

World climatic regions and their problems (Gg2, 5) Atlases that show climatic regions would be useful. Encourage the children to discuss in groups the problems that may be encountered in each region.

❏ As an individual or class activity, challenge the children to make lists of the ways in which the various climatic problems might be solved.

The world's rainfall (Ma5/3; Gg2) Atlases will be needed for this activity. The sheet may encourage discussions about how water shortages might be dealt with and water supplies in various countries.

Plants and animals

Alphabet dot-to-dot (En2/1, 2/2) This activity will help to familiarise the children with the alphabet in lower and upper case. Reference books may be needed to find out the animals' names (hawksbill turtle and snow leopard).

Number dot-to-dot (Ma2/2) Stress the importance of joining up the dots/answers in the correct order. Reference books may be needed to find out the animal's name (black rhinoceros).

Endangered species jigsaw If the jigsaw is stuck on to card, coloured in and covered with clear, self-adhesive plastic film before being cut into pieces, it will make a longer-lasting puzzle. The animals shown are: panda, African elephant, black rhinoceros, mountain gorilla, scarlet macaw, manatee, blue whale, rabbit-bandicoot.

❏ Let the children draw their own pictures which could be cut up to make puzzles.

Planning a wildlife area (Gg1/2; Sc2/2) It will be necessary to discuss the importance of placing particular plants in sunny spots and the siting of the pond away from too many trees so that it does not become full of dead leaves.

❏ Make the activity more relevant by planning something similar for your own school. This could involve choosing where to put plants in a classroom or corridor, if an outdoor site is unavailable.

Design a T-shirt (Te2, 3, 4) Provide some real T-shirts with environmental themes for the children to look at. Discuss the importance of clear labelling, use of colours and so on.

❏ If possible, provide the children with fabric crayons or paints with which to copy their designs on to real T-shirts. Alternatively, they could copy their designs on to life-size cardboard T-shirt shapes for a wall display.

Caring for our wildlife (En2/3) This activity aids familiarity with wildlife words and the use of dictionaries. The words could form a useful word bank for work on this topic.

Protecting our wildlife (En3) Begin by discussing the children's ideas and experiences on the subject and read some extracts from suitable

books. The word bank will be useful for spelling and to stimulate the children's writing.

'Saving our plants and animals' writing paper (En3) This page allows the children to write their own stories or information about the topic. The attractive border will encourage the children to produce work to be displayed.

Extinct animals (En2/3, 2/4; Sc2/2) This activity encourages the use of reference materials.

❏ Encourage the children to find out about other animals that have become extinct.

Endangered animal species (En2/2, 2/3; Sc2/2) This task encourages the children to use reference books and to summarise the information they find.

❏ Ask the children to find out about endangered species in this country. Discuss ways of ensuring they do not become extinct.

Animals at risk (En2/2, 2/3; Sc2/4, 2/5) Appropriate reference materials are essential for this activity and class or group discussions may be necessary to elicit possible ways to save endangered species.

❏ Ask the children to list other animals 'at risk'.

Threats to wildlife (Sc2/4, 2/5) This activity is designed to make the children aware of the damage that everyday wastes can have on wildlife. Share ideas through group discussions.

Save for a good cause (Ma4/4) This page could be enlarged on a photocopier. Photocopy on to thin card or stick the net of the box on to card.

Animal alliteration (En3) This activity encourages experimentation with words and the use of a dictionary. Whole class or group practice may be needed initially.

What do plants need? (Sc1/2, 1/3, 2/2, 2/3) It may be necessary to continue this experiment for several weeks, for which the children could devise their own record sheet.

❏ After completing the experiment, tell the children to summarise their results as a description of how to care for plants. They could also write, or discuss, how to care for bigger plants and trees.

❏ Experiment with different seed types. Do different plants need different conditions for growth? Try growing seedlings outside, in various conditions, and compare them with the ones grown indoors.

In the zoo (Gg1/2, 1/3) This sheet provides practice with compass directions. The result being that Graham should meet Marilyn by the penguin pool.

❏ Make maps of the school or local area and find the most direct route between two points. This could be related to fuel economy for commercial vehicles, for example, and could be reinforced by the activity 'Saving fuel' (page 35).

What do you think? (En1, 3) Encourage group discussion. Provide reference materials so that the children's views can be substantiated.

❏ Base a class debate on one of these issues.

Our effect on wildlife (En2, 3) Provide reference materials to help the children complete this puzzle. *Across:* 1 mountain gorilla; 5 whale; 6 elephant; 8 snake; 9 macaw.
Down: 2 rhinoceros; 3 snow leopard; 4 turtle; 7 panda.

❏ Let the children devise their own endangered animal crossword puzzles.

Detecting pollution (Sc2/5) Lichens also grow on stone walls and trees. Encourage the use of hand lenses and field guidebooks for more exact identification.

Endangered species around the world (Gg1/4; En2/4) Reference books and atlases will be needed for this activity.

❏ Why are these animals endangered?

Fact or opinion? (En1) Discuss the difference between a 'fact' and an 'opinion'. This activity should provide a good stimulus for class and group debates.

Food chains (Sc2/4) Discuss how the level of pollutants in the animals at the top of the chain rises because they have eaten animals already contaminated and how the pollution could be prevented.

❏ Can the children produce other food chains and suggest possible pollutants in these chains?

Tropical rainforests (Gg1/3, 1/4; En2/4) Provide atlases and reference books for this task. The countries with rainforests are:
G = Guatemala; E = El Salvador; N = Nicaragua;
C = Costa Rica; B = Belize; Co = Colombia;
Br = Brazil; U = Uruguay; A = Africa;
M = Madagascar; I = India;
My = Myanma (Burma); V = Vietnam;
P = Philippines; T = Thailand; S = Sumatra;
J = Java; Sa = Sarawak and Borneo;
Su = Sulawesi; Pa = Papua New Guinea;
Au = Australia; Ja = Japan.

❏ Discuss with the children why they think rainforests occur in these areas.

Conservation projects (Gg1/4; En2, 3) The national parks and reserves listed are found in: USA (Yellowstone), UK (Snowdonia), Tanzania (Serengeti), Peru (Manu), Brazil (Amazonia), Australia (Ayers Rock), South Africa (Pilanesberg), China (Poyang Hu), Spain (Coto Donana), Kenya (Masai Mara), Japan (Kushiro), Nigeria (Yankari), Canada (Jasper/Banff), India (Kanha), Greenland (North-east Greenland), Russia (Taimyr).

❏ Encourage the children to find out why Antarctica was considered important enough to protect through a treaty between 13 countries, which countries signed the treaty, and whether or not this protection has been successful.

What are these things made from?

❖ Match each raw material on the top row with the correct end product on the bottom row.

tree

corn

iron ore

coal

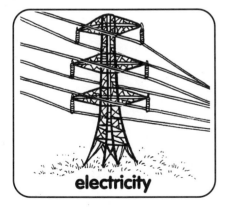
electricity

newspaper

cooking oil

steel screw

❖ Find out what a window, some curtains and a brick are made from.

Natural resources

Natural resources

✤ Match each of these natural resources with the way it might be used.

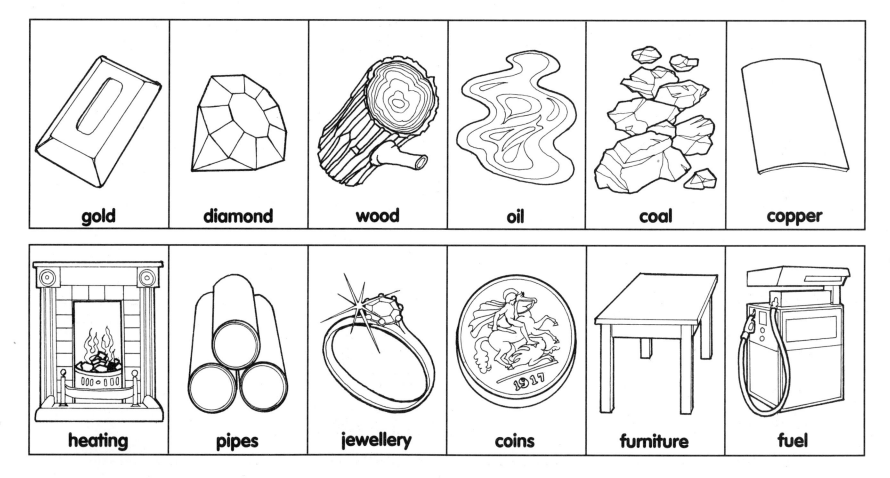

gold   diamond   wood   oil   coal   copper

heating   pipes   jewellery   coins   furniture   fuel

✤ Find out what iron, tin, water, bauxite, opal and slate are used for.

Making use of rubbish

✤ How could you reuse these items of rubbish? Draw or write your answers in the boxes provided.

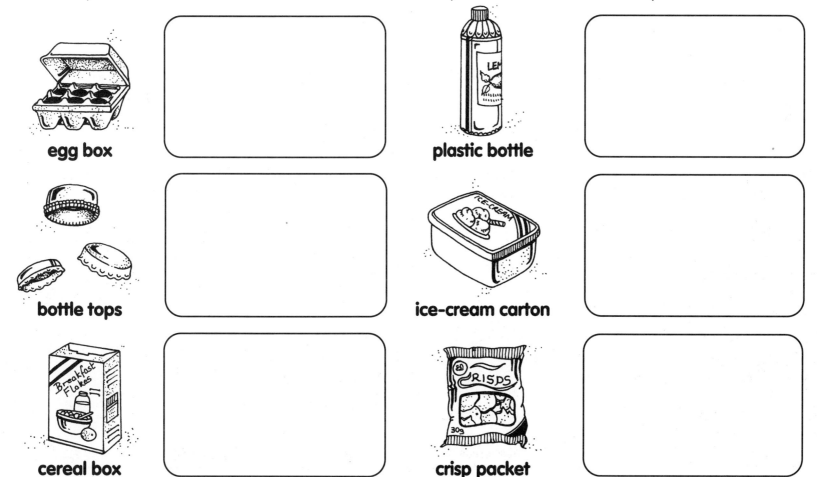

egg box

plastic bottle

bottle tops

ice-cream carton

cereal box

crisp packet

✤ Make a list of other items of rubbish, from home or school, and say how you could reuse each one.

'Our resources' writing paper

Name _____

Our resources

Bookmark messages

We can use bookmarks to get messages across.
- ♣ Colour these bookmarks, glue them on to card and then cut them out.
- ♣ Make up your own design on the blank bookmark. Think carefully about the message you want to give.

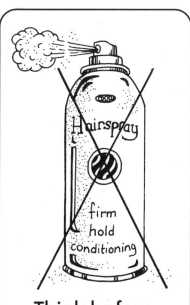

Think before
you buy!
Use pump-
action sprays,
NOT aerosols!

Save
our
rainforests!

Save our
resources.
RECYCLE!

Saving our resources

Saving our resources

✤ Complete this puzzle to find out ways of saving resources.

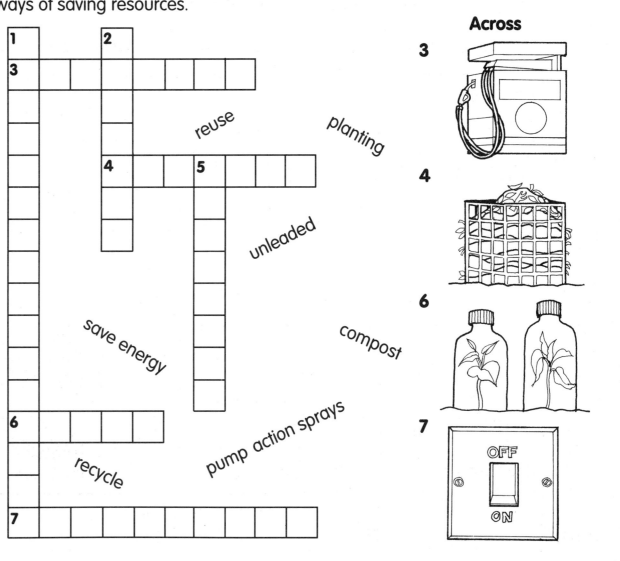

reuse

planting

unleaded

save energy

compost

pump action sprays

recycle

Down

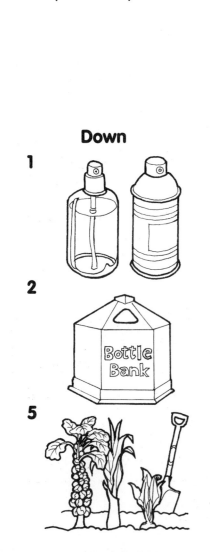

1

2

Bottle Bank

5

Across

3

4

6

OFF

ON

7

Name _____

Using materials wisely

Whether at home or at school, we should think of ways to use materials wisely, to save waste and to use resources more carefully.

♣ Think of things you should do and things you should not do when using each of these materials.

Buying wooden furniture.

Do
Don't

Using pens.

Do
Don't

Using computer paper.

Do
Don't

Empty cardboard boxes.

Do
Don't

Using envelopes.

Do
Don't

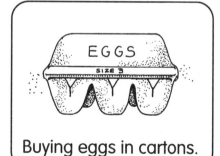

Buying eggs in cartons.

Do
Don't

Buying paper.

Do
Don't

Buying take-aways.

Do
Don't

Design a badge

 # Design a badge

✤ Design a badge to tell people each of these messages.

Save water.

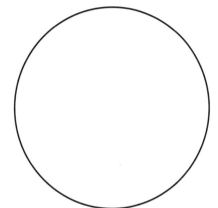

Protect rainforests.

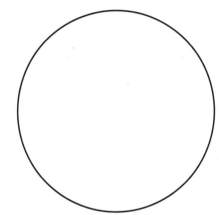

Use pump-action
sprays, not aerosols!

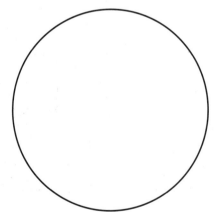

Save electricity.

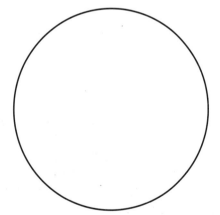

Cycle, don't drive.

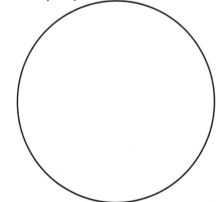

Recycle, reuse, don't dump!

✤ Cut out your badge designs and stick them on to cardboard. Fix safety pins
on the backs of your badges and wear them.

Find the resources

You will find all the resources listed below in the grid. They are written vertically, horizontally and diagonally.

✤ Circle each word in the grid as you find it.

bauxite	tin	water	wind
copper	iron	silver	uranium
oil	coal	diamond	zinc
wood	gold	sun	gas

z	i	n	c	d	e	n	t	o	z	t	w	e	l
y	a	w	n	o	e	d	b	t	a	i	e	y	x
b	t	o	i	l	a	p	x	s	u	n	t	a	e
m	l	o	a	b	u	s	r	q	p	r	w	t	b
n	x	d	y	u	c	o	p	p	e	r	l	p	n
o	y	b	z	m	a	t	b	d	z	w	y	x	o
x	w	e	a	p	t	a	n	e	w	i	l	n	s
l	e	a	z	o	n	i	m	g	e	a	s	b	t
m	n	e	t	a	w	w	b	a	u	x	i	t	e
p	r	t	s	e	a	l	i	s	z	w	l	p	e
l	p	c	r	o	r	w	s	p	l	i	v	w	z
q	u	o	z	p	e	i	r	o	n	e	e	p	b
y	t	a	e	p	s	l	m	n	y	o	r	s	t
g	o	l	d	e	b	u	r	a	n	i	u	m	s
t	y	b	z	w	o	r	s	t	u	w	b	a	e
s	t	e	d	i	a	m	o	n	d	b	d	s	t

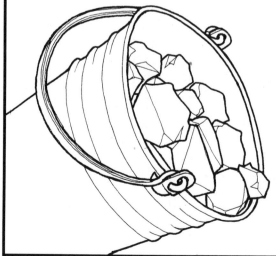

✤ Find out what each of these resources is used for and write a list of the uses on the back of this sheet.

Name _____

How green is your school?

♣ How environmentally aware is your school? Conduct this survey to find out.

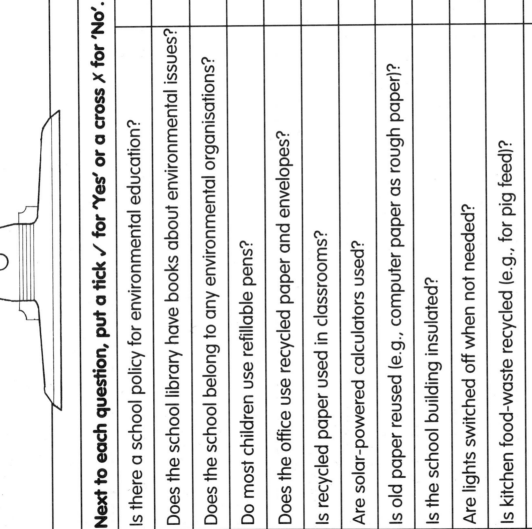

Next to each question, put a tick ✓ for 'Yes' or a cross ✗ for 'No'.

Is there a school policy for environmental education?	
Does the school library have books about environmental issues?	
Does the school belong to any environmental organisations?	
Do most children use refillable pens?	
Does the office use recycled paper and envelopes?	
Is recycled paper used in classrooms?	
Are solar-powered calculators used?	
Is old paper reused (e.g., computer paper as rough paper)?	
Is the school building insulated?	
Are lights switched off when not needed?	
Is kitchen food-waste recycled (e.g., for pig feed)?	
Does school milk come in returnable glass bottles?	
Is recycled toilet paper used?	
Does the school have a garden or wildlife area?	
Is any waste collected for recycling?	

♣ If you only have a few ticks on your survey sheet discuss with your teacher ways of improving the situation in your school. Involve the school governors, PTA and parents, if possible.

Name ____________________

My pledge to help protect the world

My pledge to help protect the world

When I shop, I promise to … ______________________________

____

____

____

____

____

When I travel, I promise to … ______________________________

____

____

When I make rubbish, I promise to … ______________________________

____

____

____

I also promise to … ______________________________

____

____

____

Signed: ______________________________

Name _____

Saving energy in the home

Saving energy in the home

✽ Answer the following questions about your home to discover ways of saving electricity there. For each question, put a tick ✓ in either the 'Yes' or the 'No' box.

Questions	Yes	No
Is the loft insulated?		
Do you have double glazing?		
Is the hot water cylinder lagged?		
Is the immersion heater set at 60°C?		
Is the pipework insulated?		
Are there draught excluders on the doors?		
Has the electric water-heater got a time switch?		
Are all the curtains closed at night?		
Are any unused chimneys sealed off?		
Is the central heating set at around 20°C?		
Is the shower used more often than the bath?		
Is there a hot water tap dripping anywhere?		
Is a plastic bowl used in the sink for washing up?		
Is the freezer defrosted regularly?		
Is the freezer always ¾ full?		
Are lights turned off when they are not needed?		
Can lower wattage light bulbs be used anywhere?		
Is the washing machine only used for full loads?		
Is the television/stereo/computer etc. switched off after use?		
Are saucepans used on cooker rings the same size as the pans?		

✽ Look at the questions with 'No' answers and suggest how the use of electricity could be improved in your home.

What does it mean?

♣ Cut out these words and meanings.
♣ Use reference books and dictionaries to help you match each word with its meaning.

✂

Land that was once fertile turns into desert.

A substance that will rot away.

Ensuring places and things are protected/cared about.

DEFORESTATION

Designed to produce more for less energy.

BIODEGRADABLE

The wearing away of land by wind and water.

DESERTIFICATION

RECYCLING

Something we use or make into something else.

RESOURCE

Breaking down waste to be made into something else.

ENERGY EFFICIENT

A resource that cannot be replaced.

EROSION

CONSERVATION

The clearing of forests by felling or burning.

Can be used again.

NON-RENEWABLE RESOURCE

REUSABLE

♣ Use these words to make a crossword.

Renewable and non-renewable resources

Renewable and non-renewable resources

Non-renewable resources, once formed, do not replace themselves (except over a very, very long period of time).
Renewable resources can be replaced.

✤ Decide whether the resources named below are **non-renewable** or **renewable** and write each one under the correct heading.

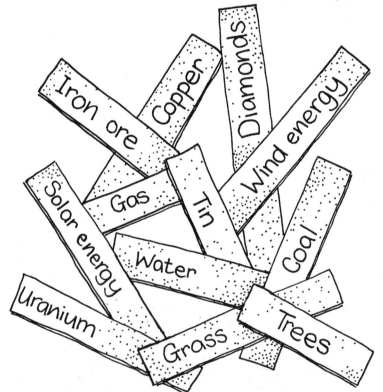

Non-renewable resources	Renewable resources

✤ On the back of this sheet, suggest ways of saving the non-renewable resources you have listed.

Make a word search

The word search below and the words it contains are all to do with materials and resources.
♣ Circle each word in the square as you find it.

♣ Now make up your own word search in the grid below using pollution or conservation words.
♣ List the hidden words on a separate sheet.

o	f	b	m	a	n	m	a	d	e
r	o	e	o	r	p	u	c	t	r
g	s	n	r	e	c	y	c	l	e
a	s	e	e	u	a	r	a	w	s
n	i	r	y	s	o	r	s	b	o
i	l	g	t	e	u	e	u	a	u
c	f	y	e	t	t	a	p	w	r
e	u	t	a	b	n	e	p	s	c
r	e	n	e	w	a	b	l	e	e
y	l	b	a	e	t	o	y	r	s

recycle   reuse   natural   supply

energy   fossil fuel   resources

renewable   man-made   organic

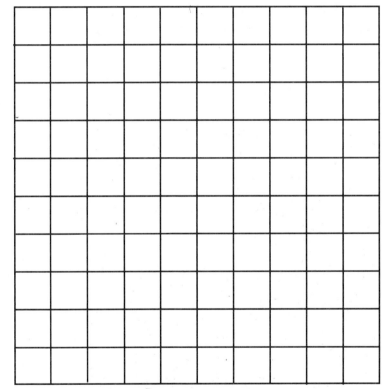

Reusing rubbish

Reusing rubbish

The following items were found in a rubbish bin: newspapers, glass bottles, tin and aluminium cans, cereal packets, plastic bottles, a broken cricket bat, cardboard egg boxes, old clothes, aerosol spray canisters, plastic ice-cream and yoghurt cartons, old toys, vegetable peelings, plastic carrier bags and magazines.

❖ Sort out the rubbish. Suggest how things might be recycled or reused. Are there any items that cannot be reused?

_____

_____

_____

_____

_____

_____

♣ Find out what rubbish is thrown away at home or at school. Are there ways of reducing this?

Name _____

 # What are fossil fuels?

♣ To find out what fossil fuels are, join up these coordinates in the order in which they are written.

- (E,12), (D,12), (D,10), (E,10).
- (G,12), (F,12), (F,10), (G,10), (G,12).
- (H,10), (H,12), (I,12), (I,10).
- (J,12), (J,10), (K,10).

- (E,9), (E,7), (F,7), (F,9), (E,9).
- (G,9), (G,7).
- (H,9), (H,7), (I,7).

- (F,6), (E,6), (E,4), (F,4), (F,5).
- (G,4), (G,6), (H,6), (H,4).
- (J,6), (I,6), (I,5), (J,5), (J,4), (I,4).

♣ Find out what happens when fossil fuels are burned.

♣ What alternative fuels could be used instead?

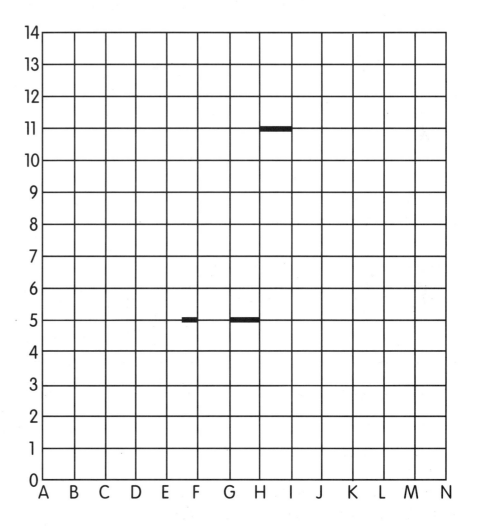

Name _____

Erosion

Erosion

Erosion is the wearing away of rocks, soil and buildings by wind, water,
ice and so on. Sometimes animals and people can wear away the land by using it too much.

❧ In the boxes below, draw the example of each type of erosion being described and then
think about what might happen to the land as a result. The first one has been done for you.

Waves crashing on to a cliff. What will happen?	Lots of hikers using a path. What will happen?	Ice forms and then melts repeatedly on a stone wall. What will happen?	A river winds its way across a field. What will happen?

The waves will eat away
the rocks, forming caves,
blow-holes and arches. _____ _____ _____

Going shopping

This shopping trolley is full of items that can cause harm to the environment.
- ♣ Find out how these items can cause harm.
- ♣ What alternatives are available for each item?

Write the alternatives in the boxes provided. Two have been done for you.

Alternative: buy loose tea- less paper and no bleach.

Alternative: buy drinks in glass bottles- glass can be recycled.

Alternative:

Tea in bleached paper bags

Drink in a plastic bottle

Carrots wrapped in plastic, on a polystyrene tray

Aerosol hair spray

Bleached toilet paper

Mercury batteries

Alternative:

Alternative:

Alternative:

Milk in a carton

Alternative:

The world's resources: 1

The world's resources: 1

Natural resources are substances people remove from the earth from which to make things. This has been happening for thousands of years, but people are using more and more of these resources and some of them are beginning to run out.

♣ Find out about the following resources. Use reference books to help you to fill in the table below.

Resource	How is it extracted?	What is it used for or made into?	Examples of this use in your school/home
oil			
coal			
iron			
wood			
tin			
copper			
diamond			
gold			

The world's resources: 2

The resources listed opposite are extracted in large quantities from certain countries around the world.

♣ Devise a key, using symbols or colours, for each of the resources listed on the table.

♣ Use an atlas to help you mark on the map (using your key) where each resource is found.

Resources	Countries of origin
oil	Russia China Saudi Arabia Europe Mexico USA
coal	Australia China India Russia USA
iron	Australia China Russia Brazil
wood	India China Russia Brazil USA Canada
tin	Indonesia Malaysia Thailand China Russia Brazil Bolivia
copper	Russia Zambia Zaire Chile USA Canada
diamond	Australia South Africa Zaire Botswana Russia
gold	Russia South Africa USA Canada

Key:

Name _____

Producing electricity

There are many ways to produce electricity, but some of them can harm the environment.
✤ Write down the advantages and disadvantages of each type of electricity production
listed below. Use reference books to help you.

wind turbines	**coal power**	**nuclear power**	**hydro power**
		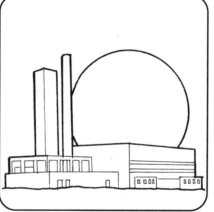	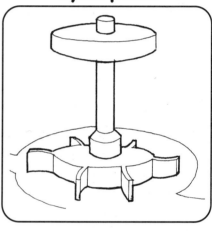

Advantages: Advantages: Advantages: Advantages:

_____   _____   _____   _____

_____   _____   _____   _____

Disadvantages: Disadvantages: Disadvantages: Disadvantages:

_____   _____   _____   _____

_____   _____   _____   _____

✤ Are there any other ways to produce electricity? List them on the back of this sheet.

Name _____

Saving fuel

The map below shows part of the route taken by a refuse collection vehicle.
The local council thinks that a lot of petrol could be saved by changing the route.

Scale 2cm = 1km
Price of petrol = 50p per litre
Fuel used = 1 litre per kilometre

❖ Find the shortest route the vehicle can take and still visit every house.
❖ Mark your route on the blank map and calculate how much it would cost.

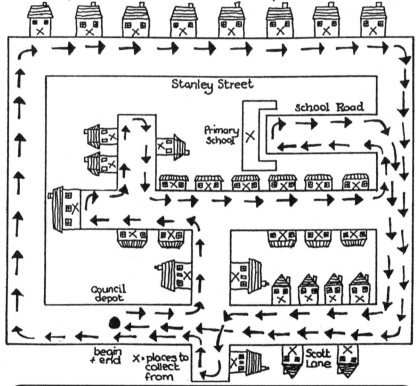

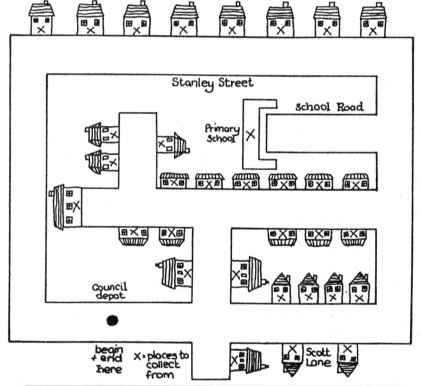

Council's route
Distance travelled:
41 kilometres

Petrol used: 41 litres
Cost: £20.50

Your route
Distance travelled:

Petrol used:
Cost:

Pollution words

Pollution words

♣ Fill in the first letter of each of the words below.
They are things which can pollute our world.

_ m o k e

_ i l

_ l a s s

_ a r s

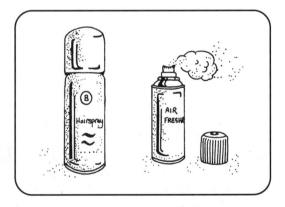

_ i t t e r

_ p r a y s

Air pollution

✤ Look at the picture below.
✤ Mark each place on the picture where air pollution is happening.
✤ Now make a list, on the back of this sheet, of ways to prevent air pollution.

Name _____

Pollution I-spy

How clean is your neighbourhood? Use this sheet to find out.

♣ Go for a walk around your neighbourhood. Put a tick in the small box every time you see one of these items.
Full marks if you score no ticks! Five or more ticks – your area needs cleaning up!

factory smoke ☐	**shop litter** ☐	**car fumes** ☐	**loud noises** ☐
derelict buildings ☐	**farm spraying** ☐	**sewage outlet** ☐	**chimney smoke** ☐
graffiti ☐	**dog excrement** ☐	**broken glass** ☐	**dumping** ☐

Teacher Timesavers: Environmental studies

Name ____________________

'Pollution' writing paper

Pollution

Name _____

Consequences

Consequences

❖ For each situation, draw or describe what might happen next.
❖ On the back of the sheet, list some ways in which these consequences
could have been avoided.

1	2
Oil tanker sinks.	

1	2
Factory allows smoke into the air.	

1	2
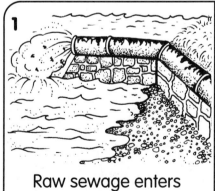Raw sewage enters the sea.	

1	2
People drop litter.	

Noise pollution

* Conduct this survey to find out how noisy it is in and around your school. At each place stop and listen and then list all the sounds you can hear.
* Finally, write down the loudest sound in each place.

Date: _____

Place	Sounds heard	Loudest sound
classroom		
playground		
in front of school		
outside local shops		
in a park, wood or garden		
near a busy road		

* Make a list, on the back of this sheet, of the ways in which some of this noise might be reduced.

Name _____

Design a 'green' machine

Design a 'green' machine

✤ In the space provided, design a machine that will clean up your local environment.

Your machine may have some, or all, of these functions:
• collects rubbish;
• sorts rubbish for recycling;
• cuts grass;
• sows seeds on bare patches of ground;
• plants trees;
• sweeps paths and gutters.

✤ Now make a model of your machine from rubbish, such as empty cereal packets, egg boxes and plastic bottles.

How people affect our environment

What effects do people have on the world in which we live?

❖ Cut out the 'Before', 'Human action' and 'After' pictures below.
❖ Match them up in the correct sequences to show how people can change the environment.

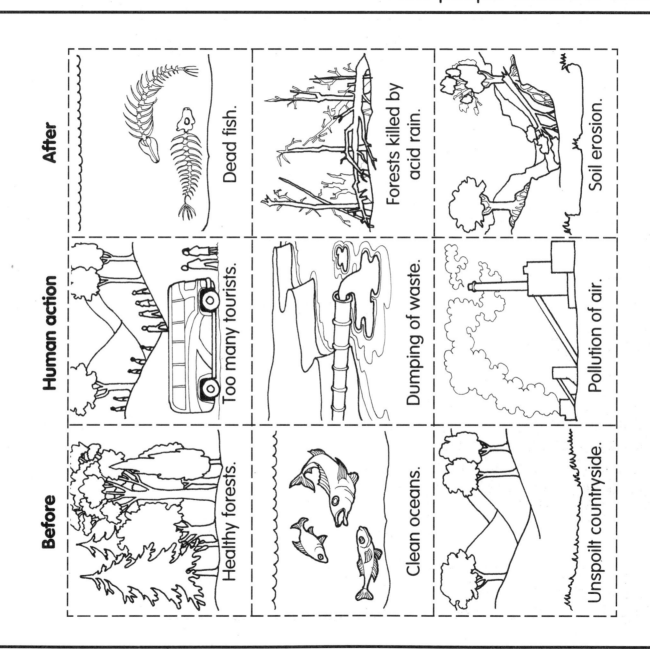

Before | **Human action** | **After**

Healthy forests. | Too many tourists. | Dead fish.

Clean oceans. | Dumping of waste. | Forests killed by acid rain.

Unspoilt countryside. | Pollution of air. | Soil erosion.

❖ Now think of ways to prevent these effects happening.
❖ Discuss your ideas with others in your group.

Design a litter bin

Design a litter bin

MEMO

Please design a litter bin with these features:

- a covered top;
- an unusual, eye-catching shape;
- a brightly coloured design on the outside;
- an easy way to empty it.

♣ Imagine you have received this memo from the local council. Use the space opposite to design the litter bin. Take into consideration all the requirements listed in the memo.

♣ Put your design on display. Does it meet all the requirements?

Journey to school

❖ Ask the children in your class how they travel to school and fill in this tally chart.

walk		car	
cycle		bus	
train		other	

❖ Use your tally chart to complete the bar graph opposite.

❖ Now answer these questions:

• Which types of transport are better for our environment?

• How many people in your class live close enough to school to walk or cycle but still travel by car?

• If cars must be used, suggest ways of using them that would be better for the environment.

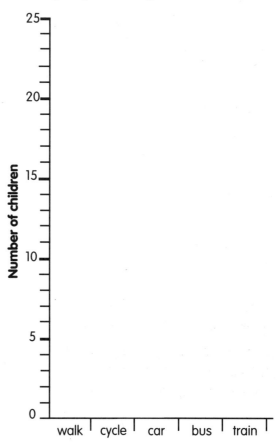

How people in my class travel to school

Traffic survey: 1

Traffic survey: 1

♣ Conduct a survey of the traffic near your school.
Make a tally of the vehicles that you see.

Date: _____

Location: _____

Time: _____

Type of vehicle	Tally	Total
bicycle		
motor cycle or scooter		
car – carrying one person		
car – carrying two people		
car – carrying more than two people		
van		
lorry		
bus		

Traffic survey: 2

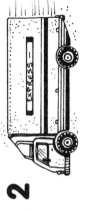
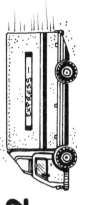

♣ Use your traffic survey to complete this sheet.

• Which type of transport is the most common? _____

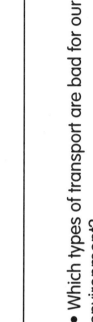

Red

Amber

Green

• Which types of transport are bad for our environment? _____

Why? _____

• Which types of transport are designed with the environment in mind? _____

How? _____

• Which type of transport is best for our environment? _____

Why? _____

• List some ways of lessening the traffic in your area. Put a ✱ next to those things you could do something about.

Name _____

Litter survey

Litter survey

♣ Conduct a litter survey of your school grounds or local area.
Record the types of litter you find by filling in the tally chart below.

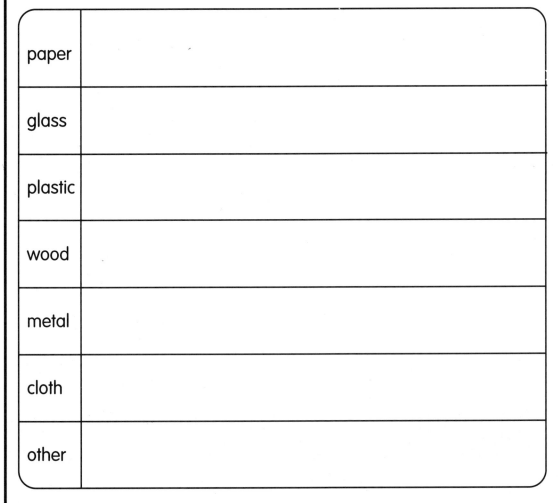

paper	
glass	
plastic	
wood	
metal	
cloth	
other	

♣ What was the most common type of litter?

_____

♣ Did you consider any of the litter to be dangerous to people and/or animals? Which items and why?

_____

_____

_____

♣ How could your school grounds or local area be made litter-free?

_____

_____

Taking positive action

♣ Write a letter to your local council about an environmental issue that is important to you, such as dogs fouling the local play area. Use the letter below to help you write your own. Take action!

(Address of person to whom you are writing.)

St Mary's Primary School,
Downtown,
Small Village,
Countyshire.

2. 9. 93

(Your school address.)

The Chairman,
Local District Council,
Small Village,
Countyshire.

Dear Sir / Madam,
   We are writing on behalf of all the children at our school who are very concerned about the state of our village playground. Since there is no fence, dogs are always messing on the grass. We think this is very unhygienic.   Also, there are no litter bins so our playground always looks a mess.
   We very much hope you can look into this matter urgently.   We await your reply.

      Yours faithfully,

    Class 5

(All sign the letter here.)

Name _____

Signs of the times

The symbol opposite is used on many packets to remind the purchaser to dispose of the empty packet correctly.

❖ Design your own symbols for each of the following:

• Recycle glass	• Bicycles only – no cars	• Environmentally safe	• Reusable

Playground litter

♣ Draw a plan of your school playground below.

✱ Mark on your plan all the places where you find litter and the location of the litter bins.

✱ Now answer these questions:

• Where was most of the litter found?

• Are more litter bins needed? Where?

• What was the most common type of litter?

• How could people be prevented from dropping litter?

✱ Talk to your headteacher about solving the litter problem.

Improving your school environment

Improving your school environment

How could your school be made a better place to be? What do you consider to be 'good' about your school environment, perhaps the flower beds or good lighting? What do you consider to be 'bad', perhaps there is no seating in the playground, not enough litter bins or too much waste in the art area?

✤ Consider each of these school areas and decide what is 'good' and what is 'bad' about each one.
✤ How might you improve them?

Area of school	What is 'good' about this area?	What is 'bad' about this area?	Suggestions for improving the area
front of school			
inside entrance			
hall			
office			
corridors			
classroom			
toilets			
playground			
grassy areas			

✤ Discuss your suggestions with others in your class and talk to your teacher about the possibility of your improvements taking place.

Design a car park

Uptown City Council has a problem. They need to provide more parking spaces in the car park without having to build a new car park. Can you find a solution?

♣ First, trace the standard car outline and cut it out. (You will need to use the car outline to see if it can move into and out of each space without hitting another car!)

♣ Now, redesign the car park for Uptown City Council.

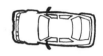

Standard car

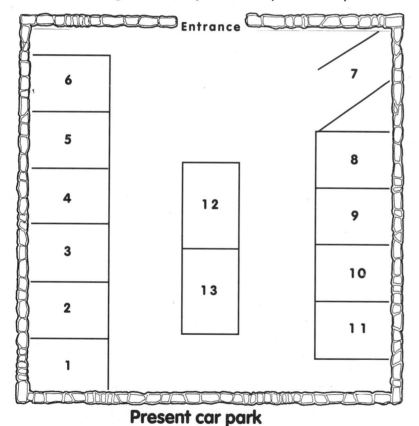

Present car park

Number of parking spaces = 13

My solution

Number of parking spaces =

Headline news

Name _____

Headline news

✤ Choose a headline from the ones suggested below, or make up your own, for the front page of this issue of *Environment News*.

✤ Draw a picture and write a report about your chosen event.

NUCLEAR POWER STATION LEAKS RADIOACTIVE CLOUD

Untreated Sewage pumped on to beach!

Child hurt by broken glass in playground

FACTORY FUMES MAKE RESIDENTS ILL

Drinking Water Contaminated PEOPLE DIE

Environment News

The paper that cares...

Issue No. 21
Printed on recycled paper

Name _____

People and their communities

Environmentally safer cars

Environmentally safer cars

♣ Complete this crossword to find out ways of using cars that will help clean up the environment.

Across

2. Encourage _ _ _ _ _ (sun-powered) cars to be built.
5. A device fitted to car exhausts to remove poisonous fumes (2 words).
6. Petrol without harmful lead in it.

Down

1. Use the car only for long _ _ _ _ _ _ _ _ (trips).
2. Travel with two or more passengers – s _ _ _ _ the car.
3. Encourage the use of alternative f _ _ _ _ that do not pollute.
4. Use the car _ _ _ _ often.

Name _____

Polluting our planet

Polluting our planet

Pollution occurs when too much waste collects in one place. It spoils the look of our planet and can be very harmful to plants, animals and humans.

✤ Think about each of these regions. What could cause pollution in each one?
(The first one has been started for you.) Write your ideas in the spaces provided.

In the soil	On the ground
chemical pesticides waste buried in landfill sites airborne pollution carried by rain into the soil	
In the water	In the air

✤ Now make a list for each region, on the back of this sheet, of ways to prevent this pollution.

'Going green'

* Find out ways of 'going green' in each of these areas.
* Put a tick ✔ in the small box next to those you intend trying yourself.

Area	Ideas for 'going green'	✔
Travelling to school		
Using spray cans		
Car travel		
Using electricity		
Washing-up		
Home heating		
Watering the garden		
Batteries		
Shopping bags		
Make-up		
Polystyrene containers		
Gardening		
Using paper		
Cleaning teeth		
Wooden furniture		
Bathing		
Cleaning the house		
Waste products		

Name _____

For or against

♣ Choose an environmental issue (such as using cars in cities, burning fossil fuels or buying real fur coats).

♣ Think of reasons for and against the issue and write them on the two scrolls.

♣ Perhaps you could have a class debate on this issue.

Industry crossword

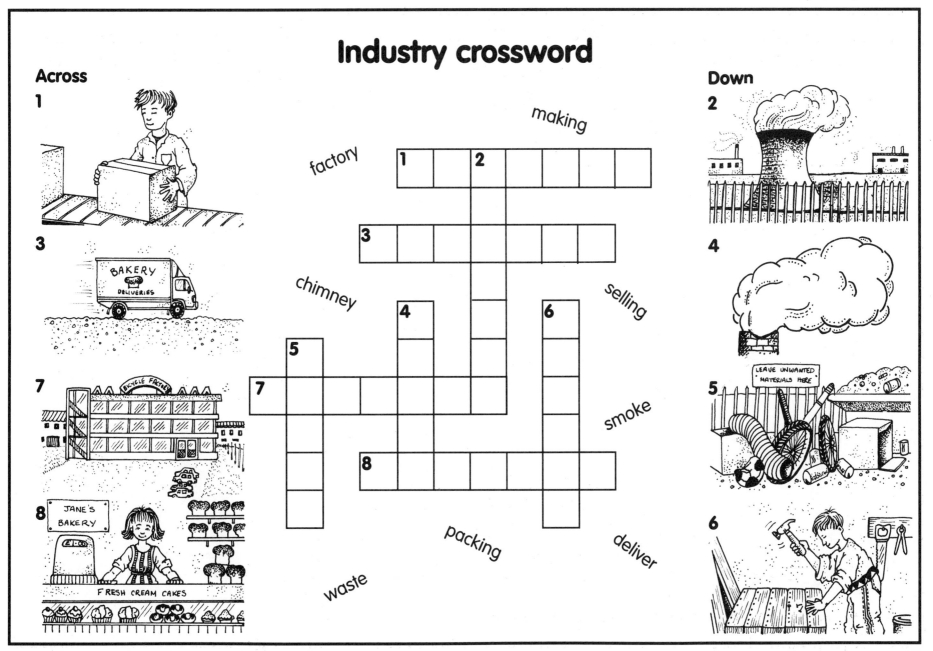

Across

1

3

7

8

Down

2

4

5

6

making

factory

chimney

selling

smoke

packing

deliver

waste

Good or bad?

Good or bad?

♣ Look at the pictures below. Decide which pictures are about things which are good for our environment and which things are bad.

♣ Cut out the pictures. Put them into the two groups: 'good' and 'bad'.

♣ Discuss your choice of group for each picture with others in your class.

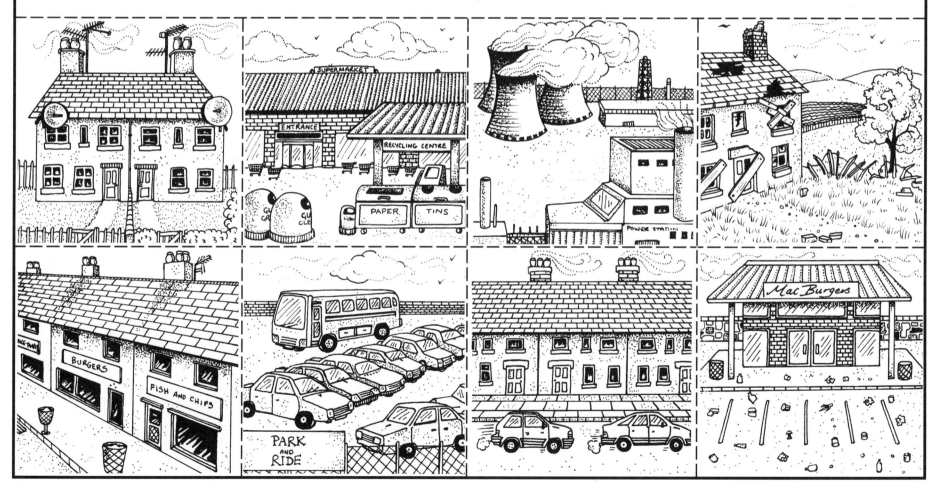

Name _____

An ABC of industrial needs

♣ For each letter, think of as many resources and materials as you can that are used by industry. Use reference books to help you.

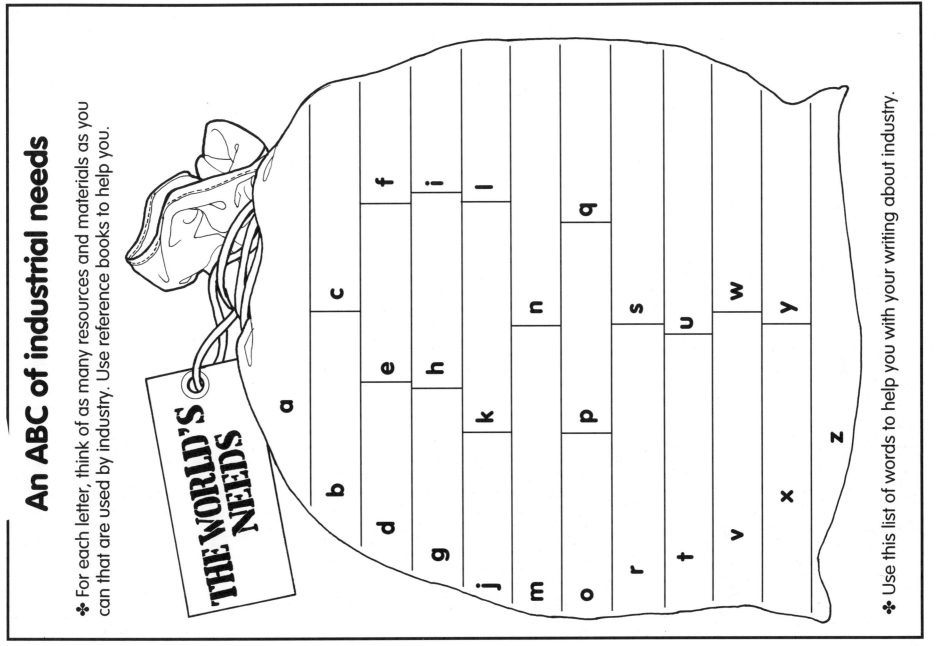

THE WORLD'S NEEDS

a

b

c

d

e

f

g

h

i

j

k

l

m

n

o

p

q

r

s

t

u

v

w

x

y

z

♣ Use this list of words to help you with your writing about industry.

New shop

New shop

✤ Design a new baker's shop to be built between the butcher's and greengrocer's shops. Remember to draw it so that it looks right beside the other buildings.

Consider:
- roof design
- shop front
- type of windows
- sign writing.

A better place to be

This street has not been looked after; the buildings have been neglected and there is litter everywhere.

✤ In the space provided below, draw the same street with as many improvements as you can.
Consider repairs, planting trees and flowers, installing litter bins and so on. Make it a better place to be.

Our street survey: 1

Our street survey: 1

♣ Complete this survey to find out about the buildings in a street near your school. Stop at each building and record the information required by making a tally or putting a tick ✓ in the correct box.

Use
What is the building used for?

residential:

office:

shop/service:

entertainment:

medical:

other:

Materials
What is the building made from?

Roof

clay tiles: _____

slate: _____

stone: _____

other: _____

Walls

stone: _____

brick: _____

timber: _____

render: _____

other: _____

Condition
What is the overall condition of the building?

very poor/dilapidated:

needs minor repairs:

good:

very good:

Improvements
What improvements could be made to the building?

new roof:

better windows:

painting:

new sign:

new door:

cleaning:

none:

Our street survey: 2

✤ Using your street survey, choose an area of the street that could be improved.

✤ In the first box below, draw the street as it looks now. Then draw it with any improvements you can think of; for example, with vacant areas turned into parks, with dilapidated buildings repaired and shop signs improved.

As it is now

As it could be

Supermarket terms

 # Supermarket terms

Many products in the supermarket have words to do with the environment written on them.
✤ Choose the correct word from the word bank to match these meanings:

• not natural _____

• a product that claims not to hurt the environment _____

• a product that claims not to hurt the ozone layer _____

• can be made into a new product _____

• can be used more than once _____

• poisonous _____

• can be taken back to be recycled or reused _____

• a substance that will rot away _____

• chickens that are allowed to live out in the open air _____

• food produced without using artificial fertilizers or pesticides _____

• a product not made from animals or tested on animals _____

• a can that uses a propellant gas _____

Word bank

aerosol

artificial

biodegradable

cruelty-free

environmentally-
friendly

free-range

organic

ozone-friendly

recyclable

returnable

reusable

toxic

Clues about industry

Name _____

The crossword below has already been completed.

♣ What you need to do is make up the clues! Use dictionaries and reference books to help you.

Across

1

4

6

8

9

10

Down

1

2

3

5

7

The crossword grid contains the following completed words:

Across:
1. delapidated
4. resource
6. fuel
8. recycle
9. toxic
10. conserving

Down:
1. doubleglazing
2. insulate
3. biodegradable
5. efficient
7. pollution

Name _____

A greener home

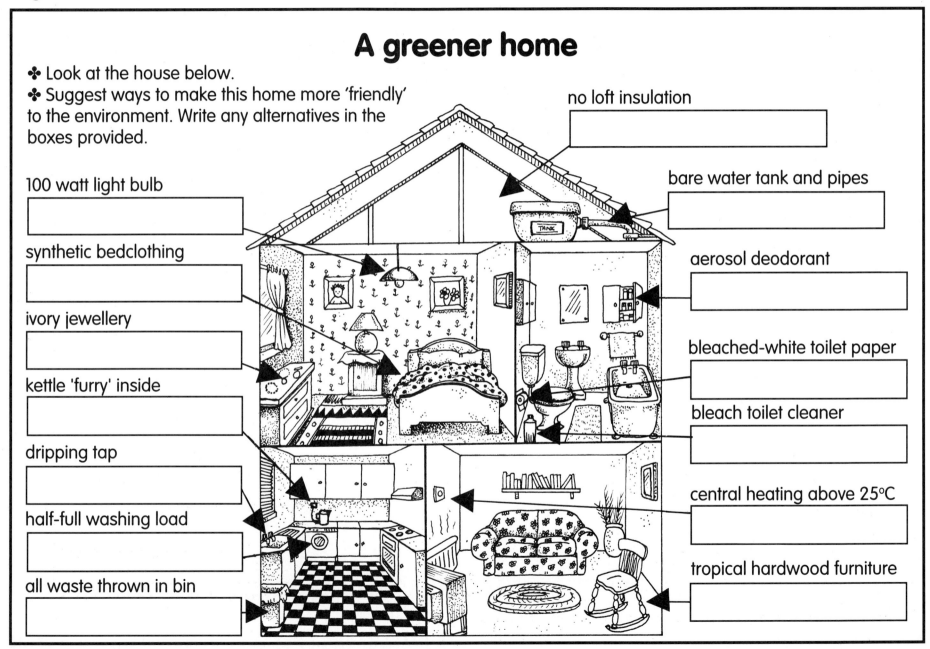

A greener home

✤ Look at the house below.
✤ Suggest ways to make this home more 'friendly' to the environment. Write any alternatives in the boxes provided.

no loft insulation

100 watt light bulb

bare water tank and pipes

synthetic bedclothing

aerosol deodorant

ivory jewellery

bleached-white toilet paper

kettle 'furry' inside

bleach toilet cleaner

dripping tap

central heating above 25°C

half-full washing load

tropical hardwood furniture

all waste thrown in bin

Teacher Timesavers: Environmental studies

Finding out about buildings

❖ Choose a building in your local area and find out the following:

• What is the building used for? _____

• When was the building first built? _____

• What materials are used for: the roof _____
the walls _____ the window frames _____

• Does the building have chimneys? How many? _____

• How many windows does it have? _____
_____

• How many doors? _____

• Has the building been altered or added to?
How? _____
_____

• Does the building have any special
features? List them below. _____

_____

_____

• Draw a window here:

• Draw the front door here:

• Is the building detached,
semi-detached or terraced?

_____

• Can you see where any repairs
or improvements are needed?

_____

_____

❖ On a separate piece of paper, make a sketch of the building.

Name _____

Is it biodegradable? 1

Is it biodegradable? 1

  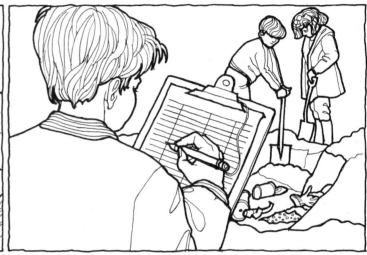

Rubbish is biodegradable if it can be broken down by bacteria in the soil. Some things will rot away and eventually disappear, but other things take years to decay and some things never do.

✣ Find out if the waste from your school or home is biodegradable by carrying out this experiment. Bury the following things under the ground and dig them up once a week to observe signs of decay: aluminium can, steel can, cardboard toilet roll tube, writing paper, cotton cloth, woollen cloth, plastic bag, crisp packet, apple core and a nail.

✣ Record your observations on the table provided on sheet 2.

✣ Continue your observations over several months, if possible.

✣ Test other objects.

Recycle
non-biodegradable
rubbish whenever
possible.

Is it biodegradable? 2

♣ Record your predictions and the results of your experiment in the table below.

Object	Prediction – will it rot?	Observations				
		Week 1	Week 2	Week 3	Week 4	Week 5
aluminium can						
steel can						
toilet roll tube						
paper						
cotton cloth						
woollen cloth						
plastic bag						
crisp packet						
apple core						
nail						

Name _____

Streets of change

Streets of change

1900

1993

MILTON STREET

❖ Look at the two pictures above.

❖ How have streets changed since 1900? Note your ideas on the back of this sheet and then discuss the following questions:

• What are the main differences between the two streets shown above?

• Which street do you find most attractive? Why?

• What signs of pollution can you see in each scene?

• How would you improve the modern 1993 street?

• How would you improve the Victorian 1900 street?

Industry – past and present

1900

1993

❖ Look at the two pictures above.

❖ Write down any **similarities** and any **differences** that you can see between them.

❖ How has industry **changed** for the better?

❖ What **problems** could be associated with each factory?

❖ What **improvements** could be made to both factories?

Water and industry

Name _____

Water and industry

Many industries use huge amounts of water every day. The water is used to cool things, for machinery, to wash equipment, to mix in with other substances and so on.

✤ Calculate how much water is needed to produce these amounts of each product. Use the table opposite to help you.

Amount of water needed to make 1 tonne of product	
steel	45,000 litres
paper	90,000 litres
synthetic fabrics	140,000 litres
baking	4,000 litres
vegetable canning	10,000 litres
sugar refining	8,000 litres
chemicals	1,100,000 litres (approx.)

- 3 tonnes of paper? [_____ litres]

- 5 tonnes of steel? [_____ litres]

- 10 tonnes of canned vegetables [_____ litres]

- 12 tonnes of refined sugar? [_____ litres]

- 2 tonnes of chemicals? [_____ litres]

- 6 tonnes of synthetic fabric? [_____ litres]

- 12 tonnes of baking? [_____ litres]

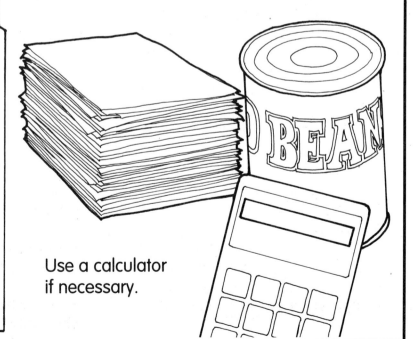

Use a calculator if necessary.

How industry can affect the land

Extractive industries, such as mining, can totally change the landscape.

❖ Look at the drawings below. They show the same area before mining began, during mining and after the mining company left. Think about the animals and people who live in the area.

❖ On the back of this sheet, answer the questions given below each picture.

Before mining

During mining

After mining

• Would this area have a lot of jobs for people?

• What kinds of animals might live here?

• What do you like about this area?

• What changes have taken place?

• How might the changes affect the wildlife in the area?

• What are the good things about mining?

• What changes did the mining company make when they finished mining?

• Is the first drawing or the last one better for animals and people? Give your reasons why.

Name _____

Become a town planner

Could you plan an ideal town?
♣ Draw each of the objects and buildings in the key on to the map.
♣ Think carefully about where things should be located. You can use any symbol more than once. Does your plan consider the environment?

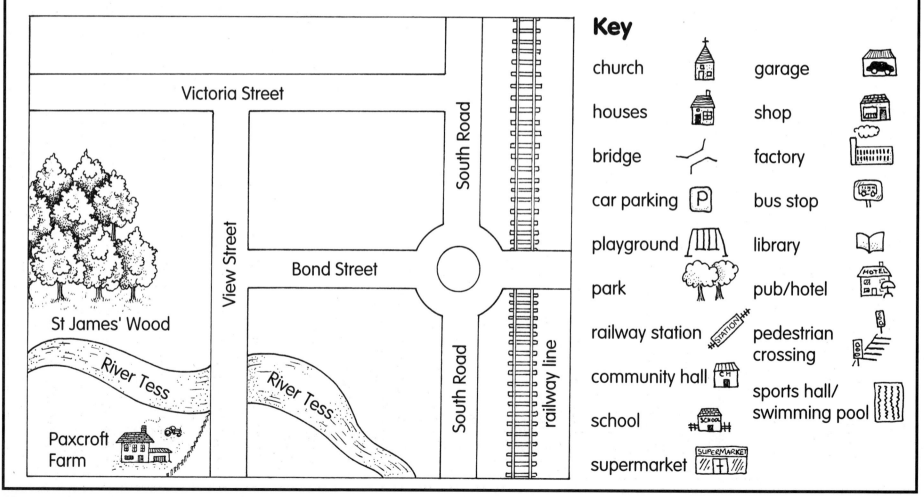

Interview a shopkeeper

How environmentally aware are your local shopkeepers?

✣ Interview a shopkeeper or the manager of a local supermarket to find out.

Shopkeeper's name: _____

Date: _____

Address of shop: _____

• What does your shop sell? _____

• Is there a car park outside the shop? _____

• Is there a bicycle rack outside the shop? _____

• Is there a bus stop near the shop? _____

• Is there a litter bin outside the shop? _____

• Do you stock environmentally-friendly goods? _____

• Do you have recycling facilities? What kind? _____

• How are goods packed for the customer, for example in boxes or plastic carrier bags? _____

• Do you sell organic produce? _____

• What happens to the cartons and boxes once you have unpacked the goods? _____

• Do you sell free-range products? _____

• Are your customers encouraged to be environmentally aware? How? _____

• Could you be persuaded to sell goods without unnecessary packaging? _____

• Are the products you use to clean the shop environmentally-friendly? _____

• What energy-saving ideas do you use? _____

Name _____

A new factory

 # A new factory

Imagine you are the owner of a new car-making factory that is to be built in the town shown on the map.

♣ Choose where to locate your factory after considering the following:

• Will you need a large or a small site?
• Will the factory need to be near roads or a railway? Why or why not?
• Factories can have harmful effects on the environment. Where would you **not** build your factory?
• How would you make sure the factory site did not spoil the local environment?

♣ Mark your factory on the map. Explain on the back of this sheet why you chose this site.

Key

bridge

house

shop

church

road

railway line

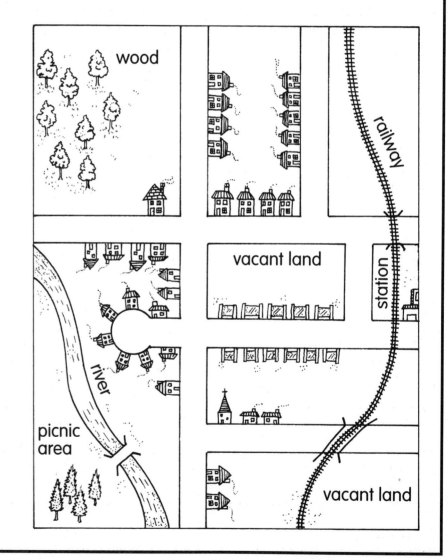

Industry – resources and waste

✤ Use reference books to find out which resources the following industries use to make their products and the wastes they produce.
✤ Suggest ways in which the waste could be prevented or reused.

Industry	Resources used	Waste created	How the waste could be prevented
fossil fuel power stations			
paper production			
batteries			
aluminium cans			
toothpaste			
polystyrene cartons			
plastic bags			

Supermarket impact

Supermarket impact

The notice shown below appeared in a local newspaper. People were divided as to whether they wanted the new store or not.

Public Notice

Rita's, the supermarket chain, are moving their store from the centre of town. It will be rebuilt on a larger site, on farming land, on the town's outskirts.

Anyone wishing to comment should write to the local council before 10 July.

P Smith

P. Smith
Town planner

❖ Read the statements opposite.
❖ Put a tick ✓ in the correct box next to those statements you think are reasons **for** building the store and those you think are reasons **against** building it.
❖ Compare and discuss your answers.

Statement	For	Against
It will create new jobs.		
Farmers will need to sell land.		
The old town store will be empty.		
The new store will be bigger.		
There will be free parking.		
Trees and fields will be destroyed.		
'Rita's' needs to make more money (profit).		
Animal habitats will be destroyed.		
New roads will have to be built.		
The site will be landscaped.		
Badger setts will need to be resited.		
New trees will be planted.		

Polluting the sea

❖ Mark crosses on this picture on all the places where pollution is happening.

❖ Think of ways to stop this pollution.

❖ On the back of this sheet, list ways in which the beach could be cleaned up.

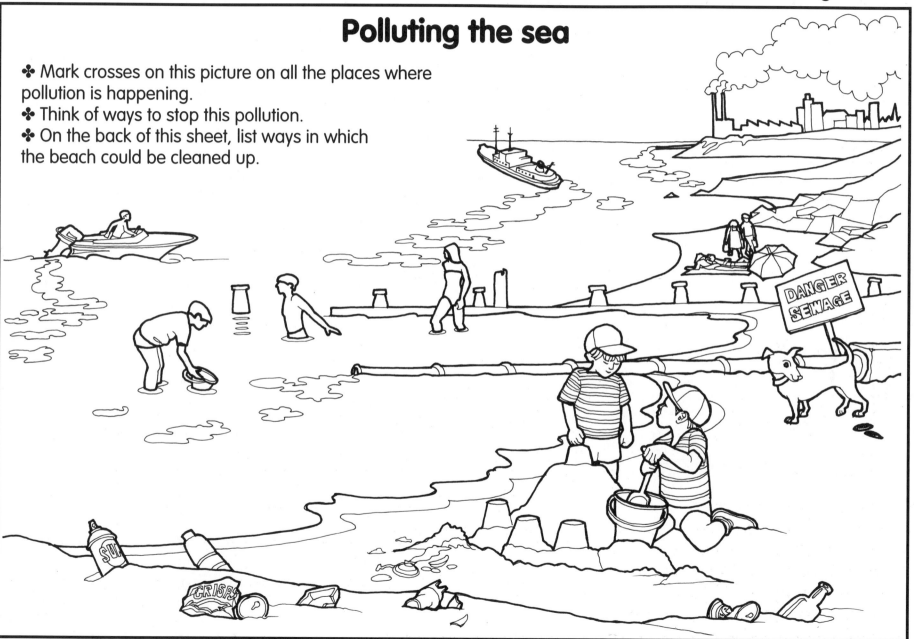

Name _____

Water – where do we find it?

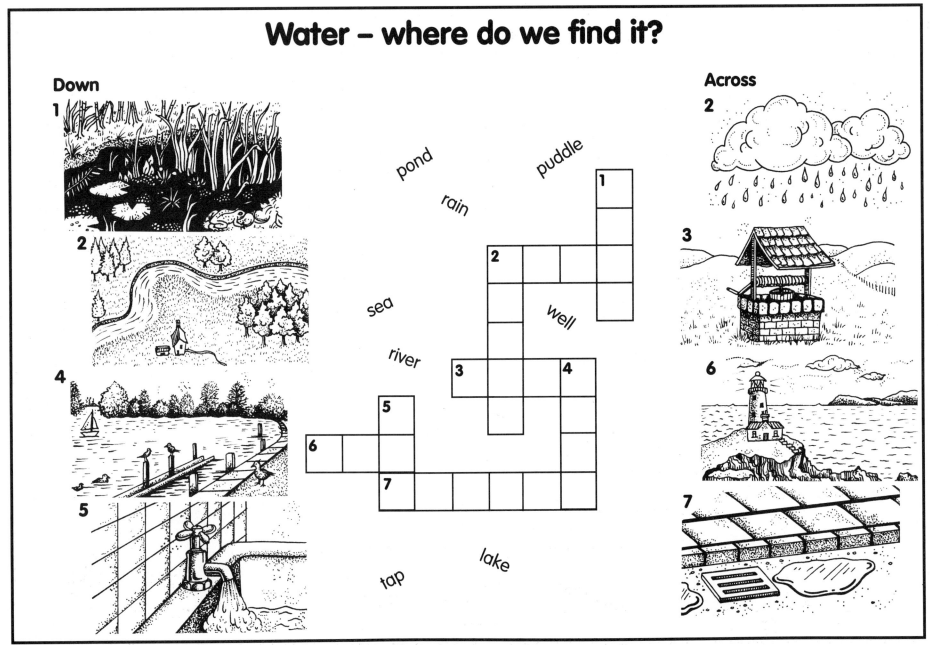

Water – where do we find it?

Down

1

2

4

5

Across

2

3

6

7

pond   puddle

rain

sea   well

river

tap   lake

Water – how do we use it?

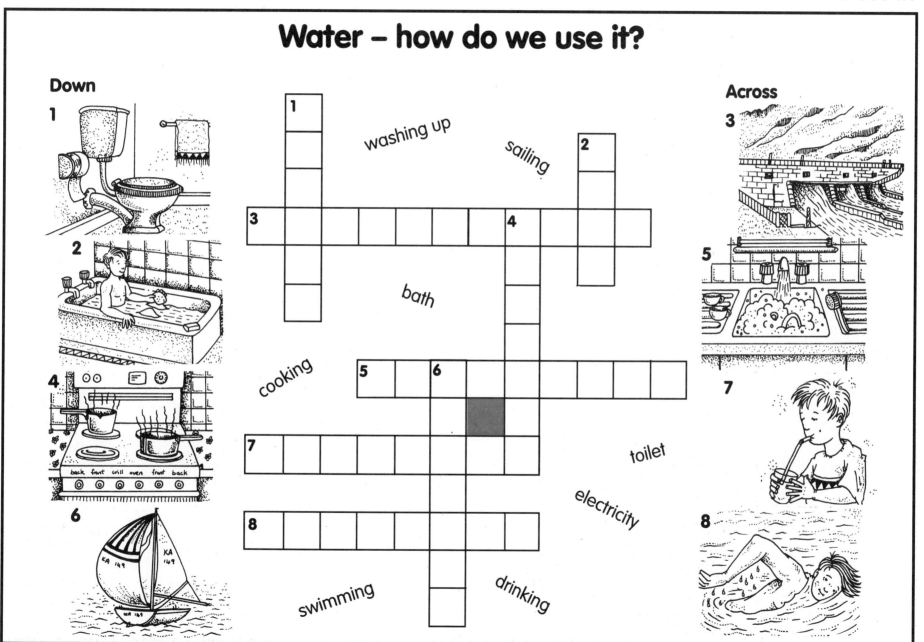

Down

1
2
4
6

Across

3
5
7
8

washing up

sailing

bath

cooking

toilet

electricity

swimming

drinking

Water – how is it polluted?

Name ____________________

Water – how is it polluted?

Down

1

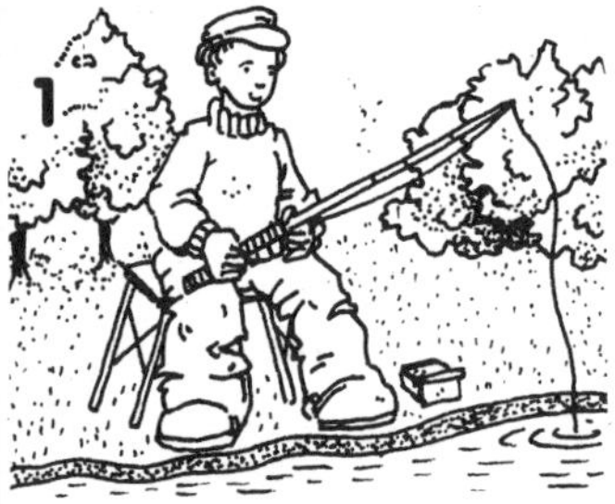

2

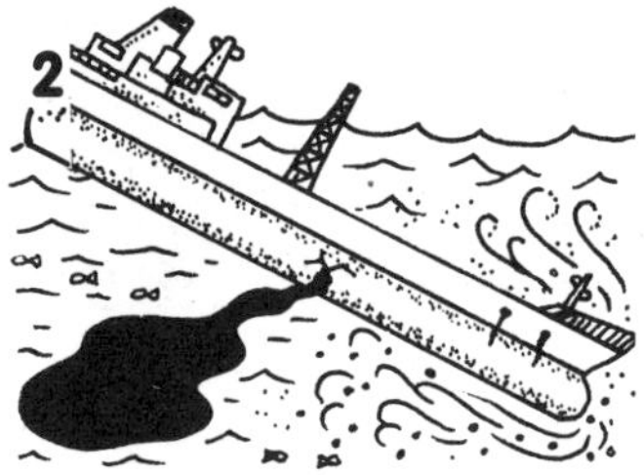

4

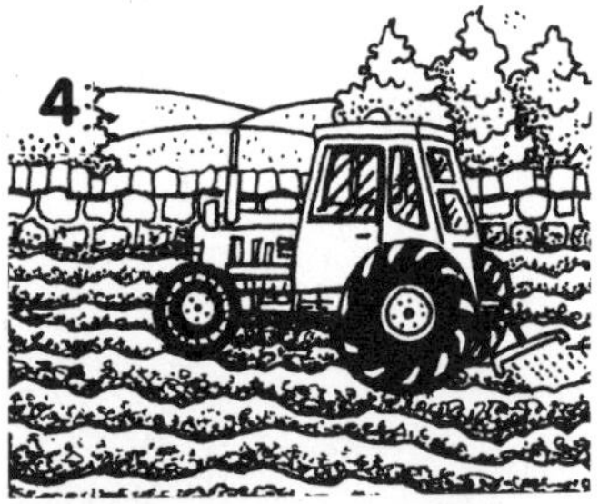

6

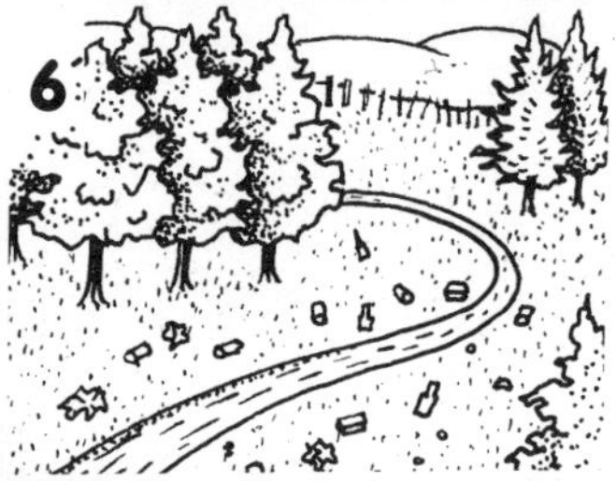

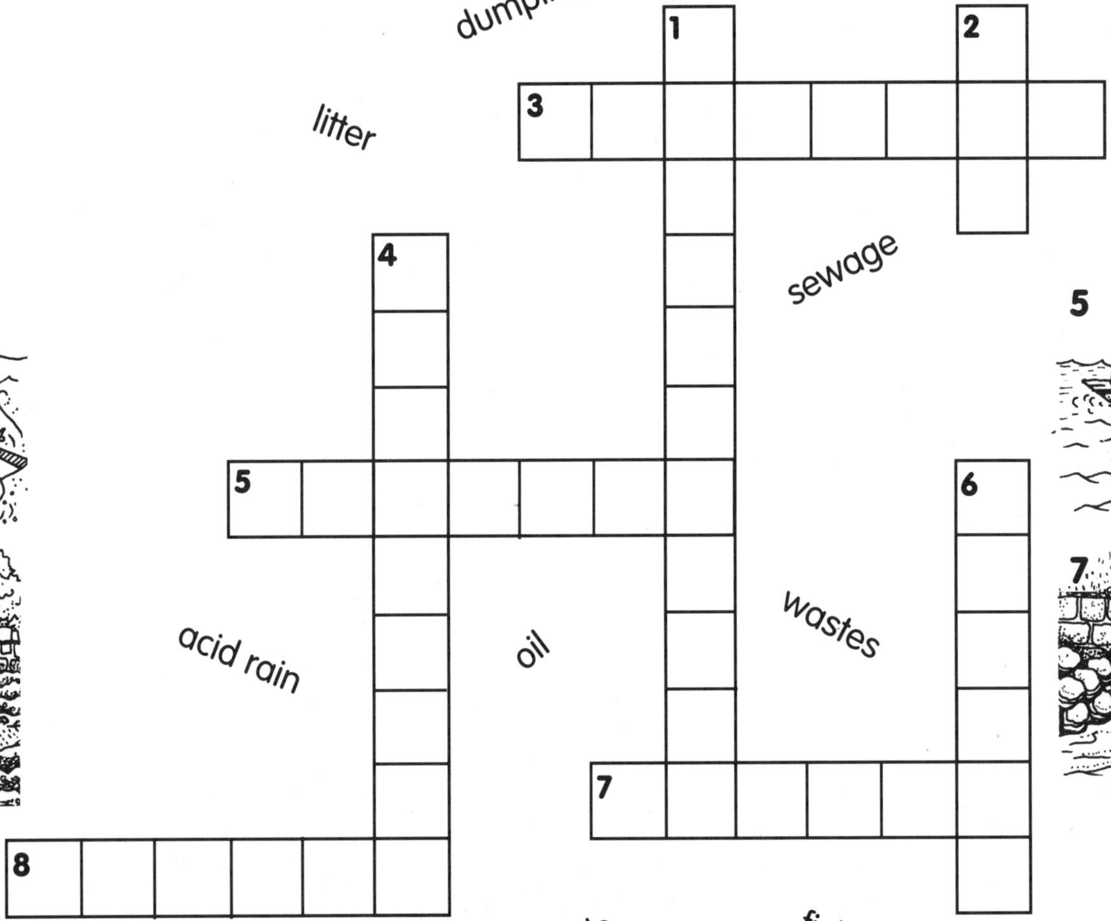

dumping
litter
sewage
acid rain
oil
wastes
chemicals
fishing line

Across

3

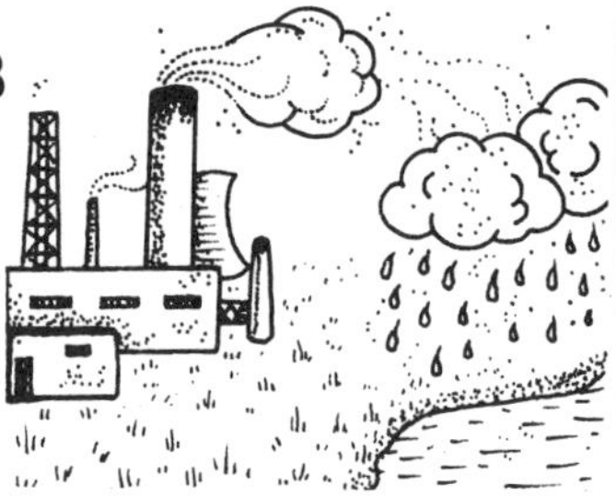

5

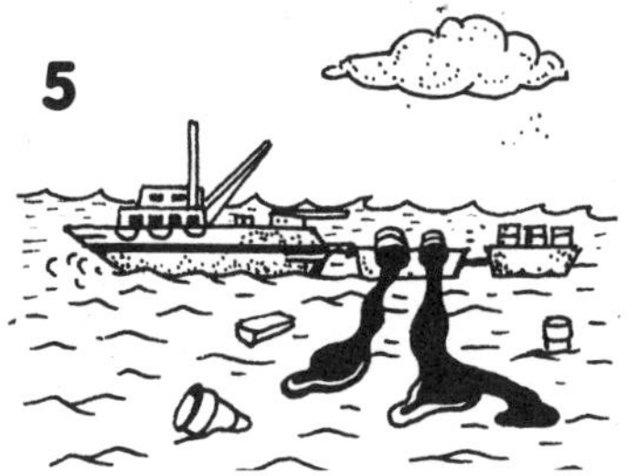

7

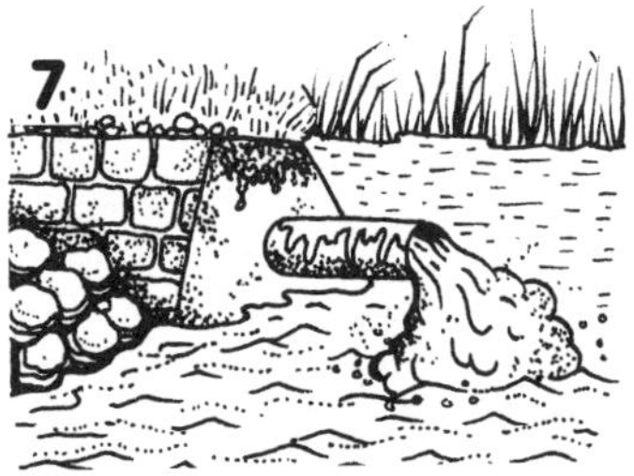

8

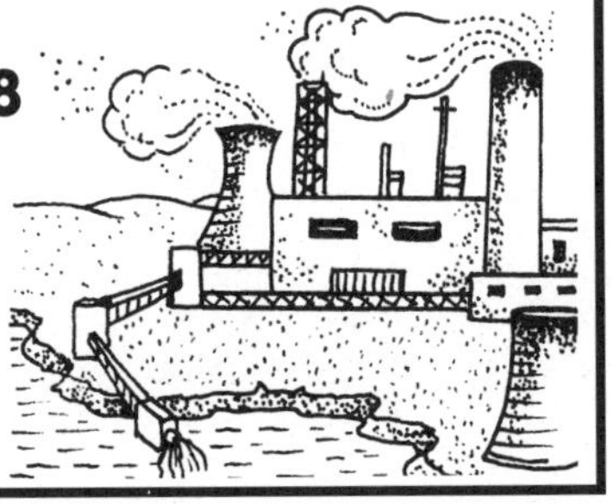

Name _____

River pollution

❖ Draw a circle round each place on the picture where pollution is happening.
❖ Make a list on the back of this sheet of how this river could be cleaned up.

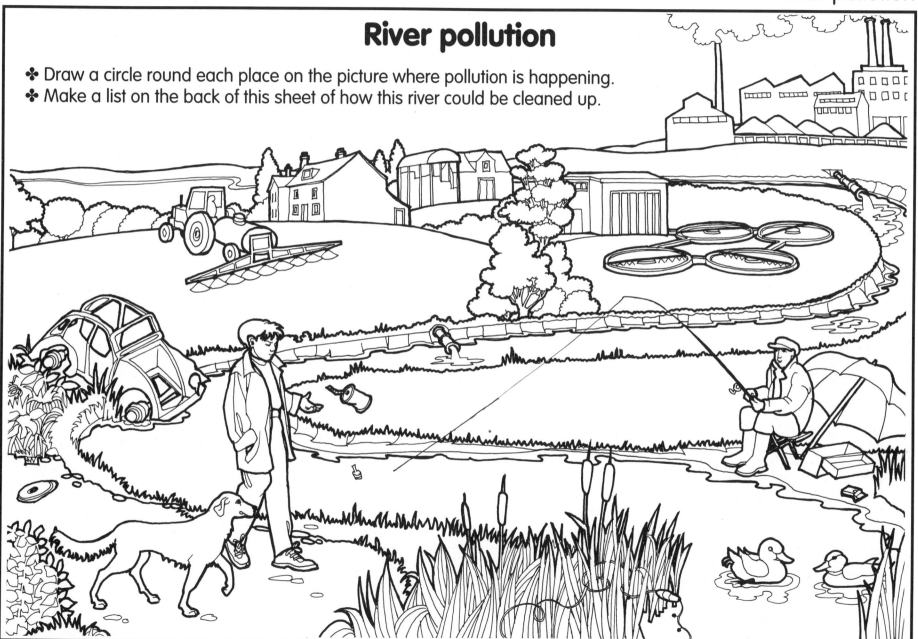

Teacher Timesavers: Environmental studies

Water – saving it or wasting it?

Water – saving it or wasting it?

✤ Sort these pictures into two groups: ways of saving water and ways of wasting water.

Putting a brick in the toilet cistern.	Having a bath.	Storing rainwater.	Using washing-up water on the garden.
Having a shower.	Washing a full load.	A dripping tap.	Washing the car with a hose.

✤ Use the saving water pictures to make a poster.
✤ Think up more ways of your own of saving water to add to your poster.

Teacher Timesavers: Environmental studies

The water cycle

+ Colour these pictures and cut them out.
+ Arrange the pictures to make a water cycle diagram. Glue them on to paper and draw arrows to show how the water moves around in the cycle.

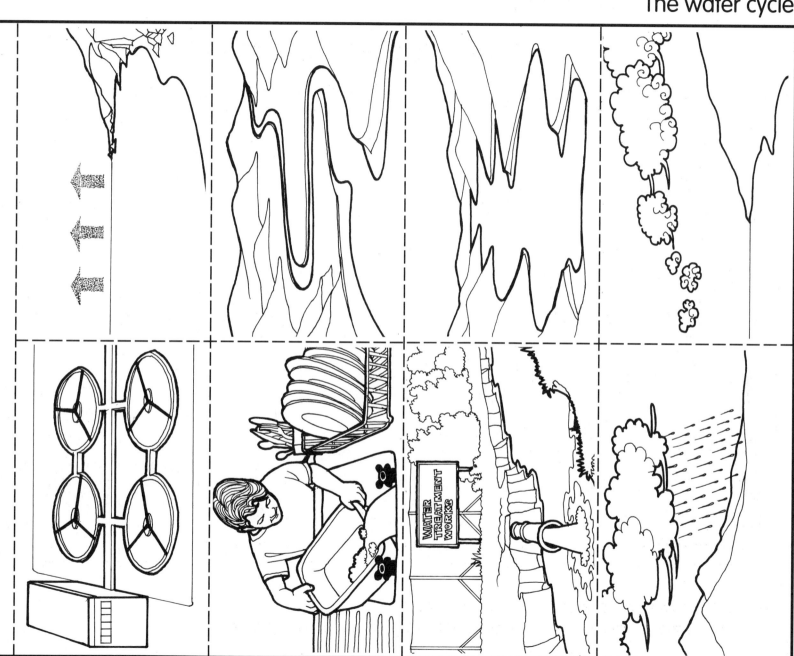

Name _____

Design a poster

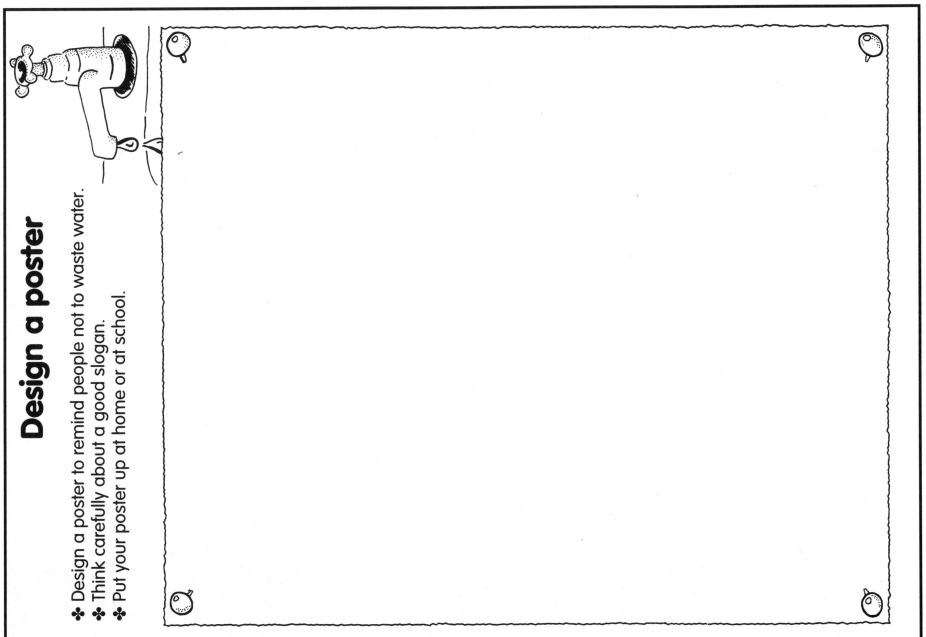

Design a poster

❖ Design a poster to remind people not to waste water.
❖ Think carefully about a good slogan.
❖ Put your poster up at home or at school.

Polluted water – a comic strip

❖ Fill in the words that you think the characters in this comic strip are saying.
❖ Now make up your own comic strip about a pollution problem.

Water words

Water words

All the words listed below can be found hidden on the two sails.
♣ Circle each word as you find it.

♣ Find out what all the hidden words mean. Use them when you write about water pollution or conservation.

Left sail:

		e	a	b				
	t	o	u	w				
	w	a	v	e	s			
a	y	e	b	s	b			
u	a	b	h	y	i			
d	e	a	o	y	b	o		
s	r	e	t	c	d	e	d	
c	o	n	s	e	r	v	e	
l	o	u	b	e	a	o	w	g
s	y	g	o	w	n	p	f	r
e	a	h	t	a	u	o	l	a
t	e	t	w	g	b	w	o	d
s	b	y	u	e	w	e	a	a
s	u	p	p	l	y	r	t	b
p	p	o	n	d	t	w	e	l
b	w	x	z	w	t	i	d	e

Right sail:

a										
b	e									
t	p	e								
a	o	u	t							
d	l	r	w	s						
c	l	e	a	n						
l	u	c	t	m	e					
e	t	r	e	t	r	w				
o	i	e	r	w	o	r	s			
o	a	c	k	s	b	t	u			
n	t	y	s	i	n	k	b	e		
w	i	c	k	o	m	s	e	a		
n	o	l	p	n	q	o	s	t	u	
v	n	e	f	f	l	u	e	n	t	x
w	e	s	t	u	a	r	y	z	k	q
s	t	r	e	a	m	c	u	t	e	n
w	b	s	r	i	v	e	r	t	w	e

conserve   pollution   water cycle   effluent   stream   hydropower   clean
tide   drought   supply   float   biodegradable   source   estuary   erosion   waves
sewage   river   recreation   sea   pond   sink   ocean

Water poems

These are shape poems. They are written to look like their meaning.

♣ Make up a shape poem of your own that reminds people to look after our precious water.

Ponds are good
Ponds are brill
They're homes to frogs
So do not spill
oil or rubbish

SHIPS LEAK DIRTY OIL
IT KILLS OUR FISH
SO DON'T LET IT SPOIL
OUR WATER !

♣ Write your shape poem here.

Match the meaning

Match the meaning

♣ Choose the correct word from the list to write underneath each of these pictures. Use a dictionary to help you.

fit to drink

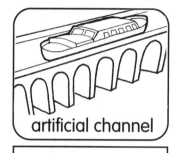

artificial channel

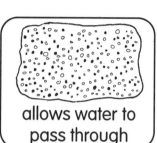

allows water to pass through

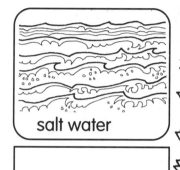

salt water

poisonous

supply crops with water

water containing waste products

area where water is stored

rain, snow, hail or sleet

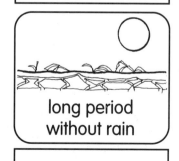

long period without rain

water that rises naturally from the ground

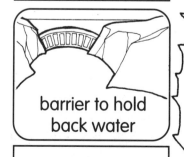

barrier to hold back water

brine

irrigate

reservoir

drought

potable

precipitation

artesian

aqueduct

dam

effluent

toxic

porous

How clean is your pond or stream?

❀ With an adult, visit a pond or stream in your area.

❀ To find out how clean the water is, answer the following questions and carry out the activities.

You will need: a jam jar, a white tray, a hand lens, a long-handled net.

❀ Now answer these questions:

• Is there any rubbish on the edges? List the kinds of rubbish.

• Is the area overgrown?

• How could the area be improved?

• What colour is the water?

• Can you see the bottom?

• Are there birds and other creatures on or near the water? List them.

• Take samples of water – is it polluted? Look for creatures that indicate the level of pollution. Then put the creatures back.

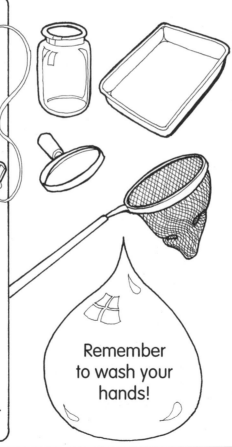

Remember to wash your hands!

Creatures that indicate pollution levels

Clean water

mayfly nymph   stonefly nymph

Fairly clean water

caddisfly larva in its case

freshwater shrimp

Some pollution

water louse

Lot of pollution

sludgeworm

bloodworm

rat-tailed maggot

Name _____

Continue the story

Continue the story

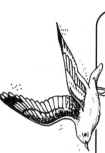

❧ Complete this story in your own words.

Disaster at Duckworth Cove

Max and Madeleine were on holiday at Duckworth Cove. One day, as they were walking along the beach, Max found a dead seagull. It was covered in sticky, black oil. 'Poor thing,' said Madeleine. 'I wonder how it died?' They continued walking, when suddenly they saw

The water game

You will need: 1 die and a counter for each player. The player who rolls the highest score on the die goes first. You need an exact number to finish and get an extra free turn if you throw a 6.

START 1	**2** Water authority test – river is clean. Go ahead 3.	**3** Healthy fish – go ahead 2.	Sewage **4** outlet. Go back to start.	**5** Clean water safety zone.	**6** Duck harmed by can holder – miss a turn.	Oil spillage **7** in sea – go back 2.
Stonefly **14** nymphs found in pond. Go ahead 5.	**13** Dolphins caught in fishing net. Miss a turn.	**12** Clean water safety zone.	**11** Pond cleaned up – now safe.	School digs a **10** pond in wildlife area. Free turn.	Polluted **9** beach. Go back 4.	**8** Clean water safety zone.
Factory waste **15** kills fish. Miss a turn.	**16** Clean water safety zone.	Water wildlife **17** sanctuary created. Free turn.	Pond net **18** digs up litter – go back to 11.	**19** Clean water safety zone.	Rat-tailed **20** maggot found in pond – go back 4.	Water saving **21** ideas used at home. Free turn.
28 Rubbish dumped at sea. Go back 3.	Canal **27** restored – go to 31.	**26** Healthy fish – go ahead 1.	**25** Clean water safety zone.	Old mining **24** area turned into lake. Free turn.	**23** Well dug in Africa. Go to 34.	**22** Dragonfly sighted – free turn.
29 Sea clean – safe for swimming. Free turn.	Frogs return **30** to pond to breed. Go ahead 1.	**31** Clean water safety zone.	Fishing line **32** and hook left by angler. Miss a turn.	**33** Corals removed from reef for sale. Go back 2.	**34** Clean water safety zone.	**FINISH**

Name _____

Obtaining water

In the past, people collected their water from ponds, streams, rivers or wells.
In some countries people still obtain their water this way. Today, in most countries,
water is brought through pipes that are connected to the taps in people's houses.

❖ Look at the three pictures below and then answer
the questions, using the back of the sheet to write on.
❖ Discuss your answers with others.

• What problems might there
be with obtaining water this
way? Would there be any
health risks?

• What problems might there be
with drawing water from a well?
Would there be any health risks?

• What are the advantages
of tap water?
• List any disadvantages.

Using water at school

❧ How much water is used at your school every day? Conduct this survey to find out.
❧ Discuss with your friends ways of reducing this amount.

Toilets

• Let a = number of children and adults in your school = ☐
• Let b = average number of flushes per day = ☐
• Total amount of water used =
(a x b x 10 litres) = ☐ litres

Average flush = 10 litres

Hand basins

Average hand wash = 1 litre
• Let a = number of children and adults in your school = ☐
• Let b = average number of times hands are washed each day = ☐
• Total amount of water used
= (a x b x 1 litre) = ☐ litres

Classroom sinks

• Use a measuring jug to find out how much water is used for washing up painting equipment and so on in your classroom = ☐ litres
• Then find out the school total
= ☐ litres

Staffroom sink

• How many litres of water does the sink hold? ☐
• How many sink-loads are washed up each day? = ☐
• Total amount of water used
= ☐ litres

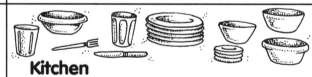

Kitchen

• How much water do the school kitchen sinks hold? = ☐ litres
• How many times are the sinks filled each day? Ask the school cook.
• Total amount of water used
= ☐ litres

Other uses

• Interview the caretaker to find out other uses of water in school.
• Add up the total amount per day
= ☐ litres

Name _____

Rivers of the United Kingdom

Rivers of the United Kingdom

When rain falls, it sinks into the ground or runs across the surface as rivers or streams. We use these rivers for many purposes – boating, fishing, drinking water, watering crops, generating electricity and so on.

✤ Use an atlas to name as many of the rivers on this UK map as you can.

✤ Mark the course of each river that you name in blue.

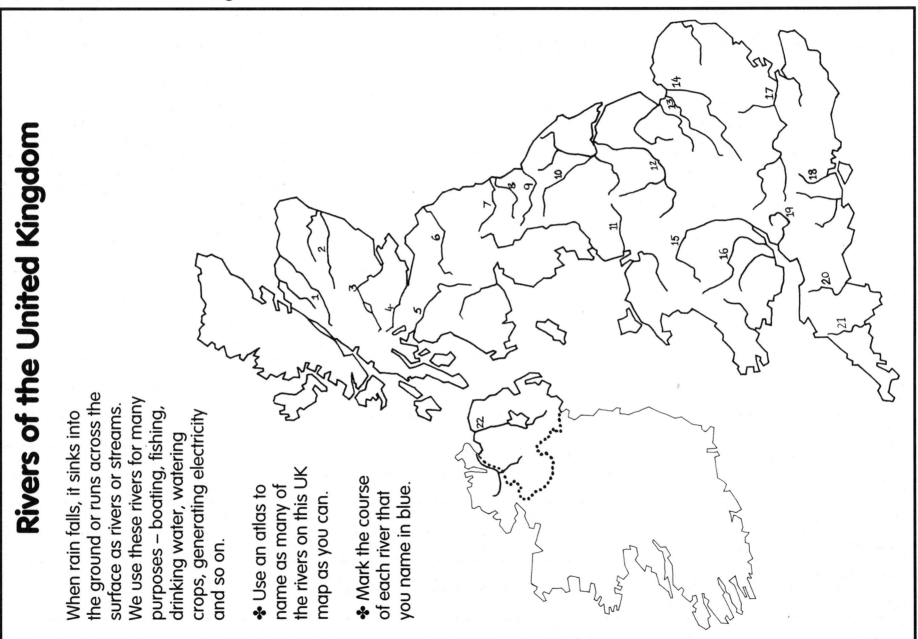

How much water do you use?

❖ Find out how much water your family uses in one week by completing this survey. Use a calculator to help you.

❖ Compare your results with others in your class. Make suggestions as to how water can be saved at home.

Activity	Average amount of water used (litres)	Number of times each activity is carried out in one week (tally)	Weekly amount of water used (number of litres each activity uses × number of times activity is carried out in one week)
flushing toilet	10		
washing hands	1		
cleaning teeth	1		
bath	80		
shower	30		
full washing-machine load	125		
washing-up by hand	5		
washing-up by machine	65		
pot of tea	2		
car wash – bucket	25		
watering garden – watering can	25		
watering garden – hose	100		
other			
Total			

Uses of water

Name _____

Uses of water

Around the world water has a great many uses. Some of these uses cause harm to the environment.

❖ Use an atlas to help you find out which country is depicted in each drawing.
❖ Then decide if the particular use of water shown causes harm to the environment or not. The first one has been done for you.

Use: irrigation near River Nile.	Use: electricity dam on the Tennessee River.	Use: sewage outlet on River Thames.	Use: sea-fishing near Lima.	Use: surfing on Bondi Beach.
Country: Egypt	Country:	Country:	Country:	Country:
~~Harm~~/no harm	Harm/no harm	Harm/no harm	Harm/no harm	Harm/no harm
Use: rice paddy-field near Bangkok.	Use: factory cooling tower, Frankfurt.	Use: cargo ship on River Seine.	Use: using well-water to drink near Khartoum.	Use: factory waste outlet on Hudson River.
Country:	Country:	Country:	Country:	Country:
Harm/no harm	Harm/no harm	Harm/no harm	Harm/no harm	Harm/no harm

Teacher Timesavers: Environmental studies

Name _____

Who has clean water to drink?

In many countries the people do not have safe, clean water
and can become sick and may die if they drink the water.

♣ Look at the world map below.

♣ Use an atlas to find
out the names of the
countries where few
people have clean
water.

♣ List these countries on
the back of this sheet.
(There are 40.)

♣ Find out what could
be done to help improve
the water supply in
these countries.

Name _____

Weather crossword

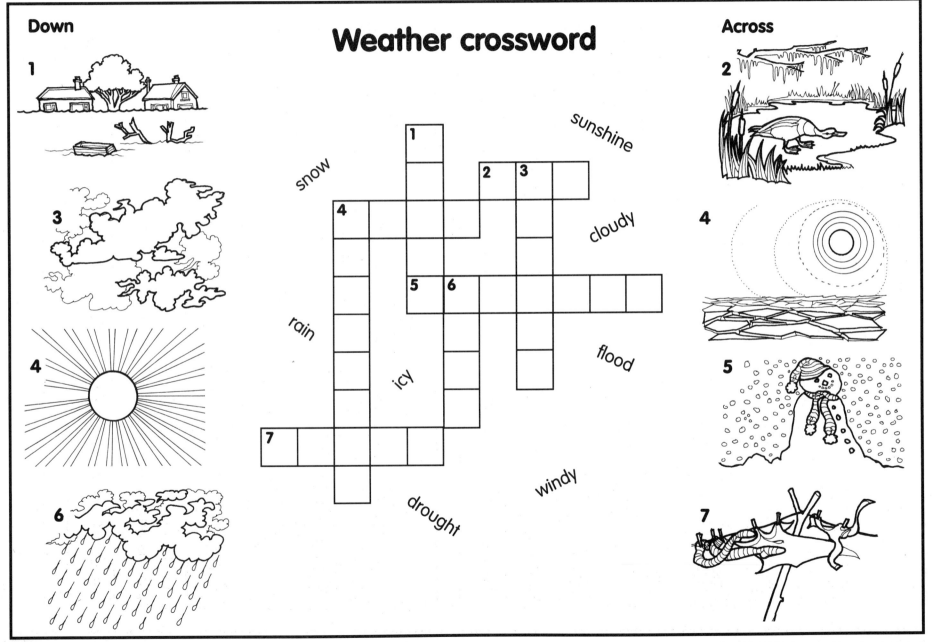

Down

1

3

4

6

Weather crossword

snow

sunshine

cloudy

rain

icy

flood

windy

drought

Across

2

4

5

7

'Feeling under the weather'

How does the weather affect the way you feel?

✤ For each type of weather listed below, write how it makes you feel and what things you like to do.

When it's raining, I feel _____

I like to do these things: _____

When it's cloudy, I feel _____

I like to do these things: _____

When it's sunny, I feel _____

I like to do these things: _____

When it's windy, I feel _____

I like to do these things: _____

When it's snowing, I feel _____

I like to do these things: _____

When there is a thunderstorm, I feel _____

I like to do these things: _____

Name _____

Protection from the weather: 1

We wear different clothes to protect us from the sun, the rain and the cold.
❧ Colour in and cut out the figure and the clothes on these two pages.
Do not cut off the tabs.
❧ Stick the figure on to card.

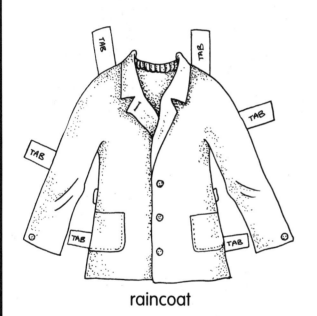

raincoat

woolly hat

baseball cap

sunglasses

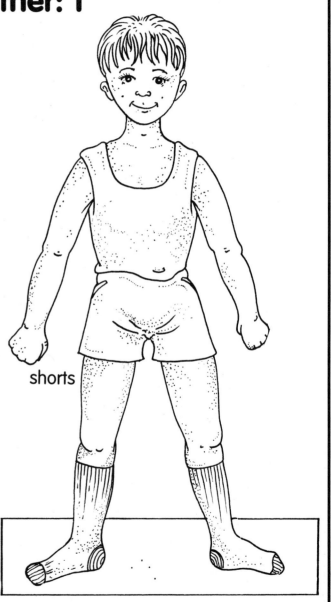

shorts

❧ Select suitable clothes for a sunny day, a wet day
or a cold day and dress the figure.

Name _____

Protection from the weather: 2

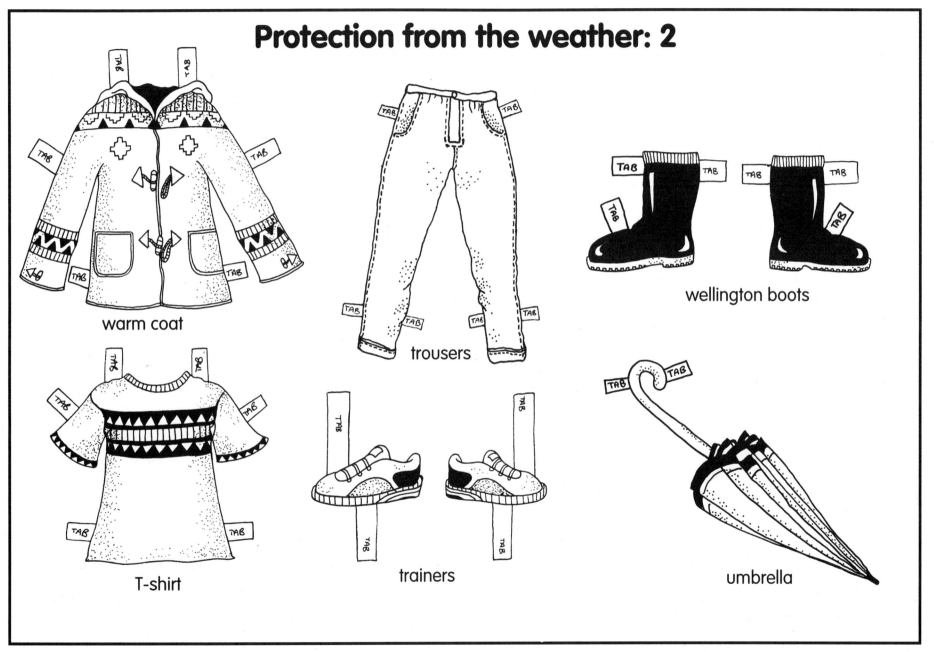

warm coat

trousers

wellington boots

T-shirt

trainers

umbrella

A change of season

A change of season

How do the seasons affect us? How do they affect plants and animals?
❖ For each season, write down how the weather affects our environment.

Name _____

	Autumn	Winter	Spring	Summer
How does it affect plants?				
How does it affect animals?				
How does it affect humans?				
How does it affect the land/soil?				
How does it affect transport?				

Protection from ultraviolet radiation

If the ozone layer continues to be destroyed, harmful UV (ultraviolet) radiation from the sun could cause skin cancer to become more common. We may need to protect ourselves more when we are outside.

♣ Design some protective outdoor clothing that people could wear to protect their skin from the harmful sun's rays, for example sunglasses or gloves or hats.

♣ Make models of your designs for protective clothing.
♣ Evaluate your designs.

Climate and buildings

Climate and buildings

Different parts of the world have different 'climates'; that is, different average weather conditions. Houses and other buildings are built to cope with the type of climate in that particular place.

♣ Match each home with the type of climate in which you think it would be built.
There may be more than one type of house for some of the climates.

house with double-glazing and insulation

house with shutters and verandah

house on stilts

house with sloping roof

lots of rain and flooding

heavy snow falls

very hot weather

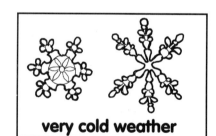

very cold weather

house built high on hillside

mud hut, no glass in windows

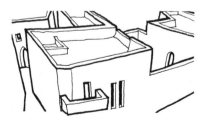

house with flat roof

house with white walls and courtyard

Changes in the weather

❖ In the spaces provided, draw or write what would happen
if there were the following changes to the weather.

| It rained every day on the desert.  | |
| It did not rain on a forest.  | |

The sun did not shine on a flower garden.

The sun always shone on a water reserve.

It did not rain on a forest.

What would happen if...?

Name _____

What would happen if...?

Changes in the climate can be caused by human actions and can have dramatic effects on the environment.

♣ Write what you think would happen...

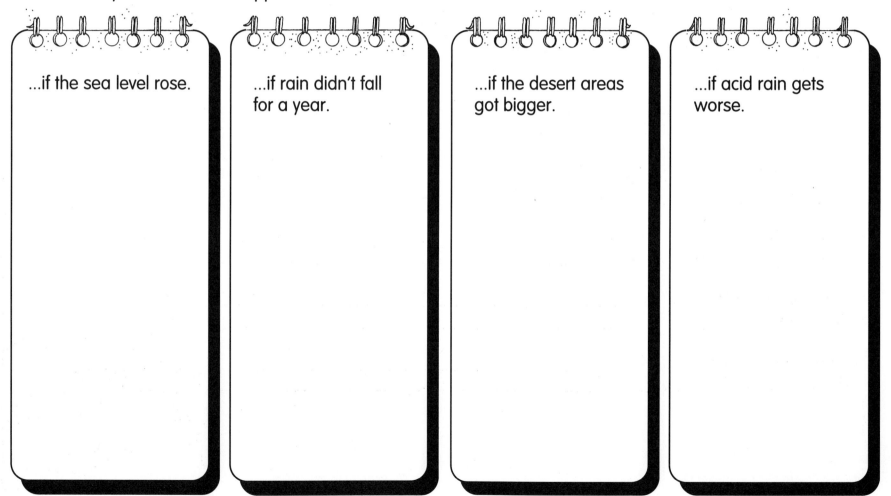

...if the sea level rose.

...if rain didn't fall for a year.

...if the desert areas got bigger.

...if acid rain gets worse.

The ozone layer

♣ Use reference books to find out the answers to the following questions.
Add the titles and authors of the reference books you use to answer each question.

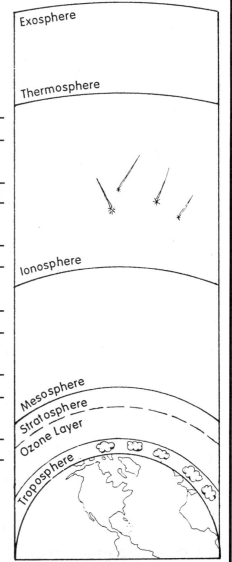

Exosphere

Thermosphere

Ionosphere

Mesosphere

Stratosphere

Ozone Layer

Troposphere

• What is the ozone layer? _____
Reference used: _____

• What are CFCs? _____
Reference used: _____

• What things produce CFCs? _____
Reference used: _____

• What is radiation? _____
Reference used: _____

• What is ultraviolet light? _____
Reference used: _____

• What is the Greenhouse Effect? _____
Reference used: _____

Name _____

Save our ozone layer

Save our ozone layer

❖ Design a poster to inform people about ways to protect the Earth's ozone layer.

You may like to include this information:
- buy pump-action sprays, not aerosols;
- take old refrigerators to a place where the CFCs can be recycled;
- don't buy packaging that is made using CFCs.

❖ Now make a large poster of your design and display it in a prominent place!

The Greenhouse Effect

❖ Read the information given opposite and then answer these questions:

• What is the term used to describe how the Earth is kept warm? _____
_____

• What happens to the Sun's energy when it reaches the Earth's atmosphere? _____
_____

• What are the main 'greenhouse gases'? _____
_____

• What happens if there are too many 'greenhouse gases' in the atmosphere? _____
_____

• What do we do which adds to the 'greenhouse gases'? _____
_____

The Greenhouse Effect is the term used to describe how the Earth is kept warm. The Earth is heated by the Sun. When the Sun's energy reaches the Earth's atmosphere, some of the energy is reflected back into space, some is absorbed and the rest reaches the Earth, warming it up. The 'greenhouse gases' in the atmosphere (carbon dioxide, methane and CFCs) trap this energy and keep the Earth warm. However, if there are too many gases, too much warmth will be trapped and the Earth's temperature will increase – this is called 'global warming'. The increase in the gases is caused by pollution in the air from burning fossil fuels, from burning the rainforests, from vehicle exhaust fumes and from CFCs, released by some aerosols and refrigerators.

Acid rain

Acid rain

Acid rain is a type of pollution. It is rain that contains chemicals such as sulphur dioxide (SO_2) and nitrogen oxide (N_2O). These chemicals are in the rain because many countries use coal, oil and gas (fossil fuels) to make energy to make electricity, to make plastics and paints and to power their cars and planes. When acid rain falls, it kills trees, wears away buildings and pollutes rivers and lakes, killing the fish.

✤ Find out about these things that will help reduce acid rain:

• catalytic converters _____

_____

• energy efficiency _____

_____

• solar power _____

_____

• alternative energy sources _____

_____

• renewable energy sources _____

_____

♣ Design a poster to warn people about acid rain and tell them how it can be reduced.

Acid rain – a worldwide problem

Burning fossil fuels releases gases such as sulphur dioxide (SO_2) and nitrous oxides (N_xO). These gases mix with the rain as it falls to form weak acid. This acid rain can kill trees. Lakes can become acidic too, killing the water creatures. Acid rain also erodes stone and brick. This is happening today, all over the world.

Certain cities are particularly affected by acid rain. There are 25 of them marked on this map by their initial letters.

✤ Use an atlas to name these cities and list them on the back of this sheet.

Name _____

What causes air pollution?

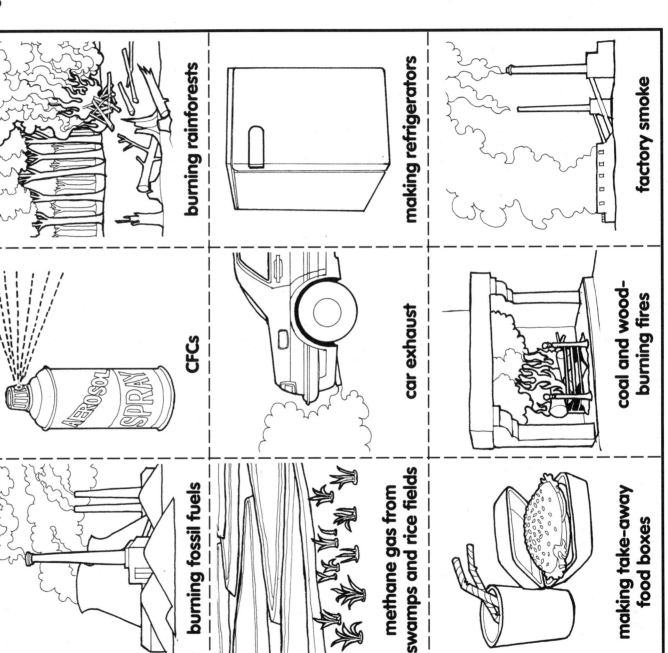

What causes air pollution?

❧ Colour the pictures below and cut them out.

❧ Sort the pictures into groups of things that help to cause:
• acid rain   • the Greenhouse Effect   • holes in the ozone layer.

❧ Do some of the pictures belong in more than one group?
❧ Discuss your choices with a friend.

burning rainforests

making refrigerators

factory smoke

CFCs

car exhaust

coal and wood-
burning fires

burning fossil fuels

methane gas from
swamps and rice fields

making take-away
food boxes

Weather word search

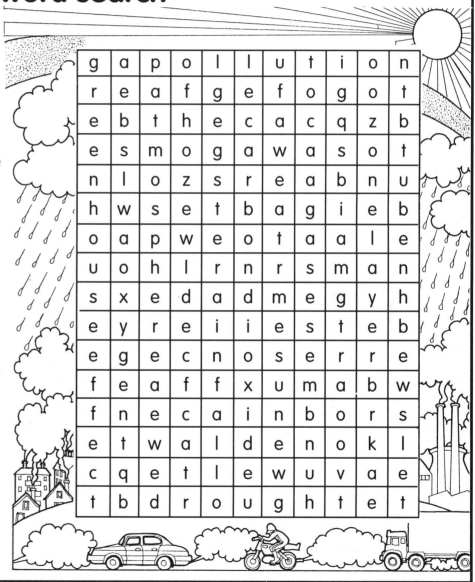

♣ Find the words listed below in the square. They are written across, down and diagonally. Circle each word as you find it.

ozone layer	carbon dioxide	rainfall
acid rain	sun	atmosphere
drought	greenhouse effect	fog
smoke	pollution	oxygen
smog	gases	

♣ Find out what these words mean and write their definitions on the back of this sheet: smog, atmosphere, acid rain, drought and ozone layer.

You will also find the letters cfc in this word search. This is not a word, it is an acronym.

♣ What is an acronym?

♣ How many other acronyms can you find related to the environment?

g	a	p	o	l	l	u	t	i	o	n
r	e	a	f	g	e	f	o	g	o	t
e	b	t	h	e	c	a	c	q	z	b
e	s	m	o	g	a	w	a	s	o	t
n	l	o	z	s	r	e	a	b	n	u
h	w	s	e	t	b	a	g	i	e	b
o	a	p	w	e	o	t	a	a	l	e
u	o	h	l	r	n	r	s	m	a	n
s	x	e	d	a	d	m	e	g	y	h
e	y	r	e	i	i	e	s	t	e	b
e	g	e	c	n	o	s	e	r	r	e
f	e	a	f	f	x	u	m	a	b	w
f	n	e	c	a	i	n	b	o	r	s
e	t	w	a	l	d	e	n	o	k	l
c	q	e	t	l	e	w	u	v	a	e
t	b	d	r	o	u	g	h	t	e	t

The world's climate

Name _____

The world's climate

What things can affect the world's climate?
✤ Complete this puzzle to find out.

Pollution of the atmosphere has caused the Earth's temperature to rise. This is called g _ _ _ _ _ (3 across) warming. The normal warming effect of the Earth's atmosphere is called the G _ _ _ _ _ _ _ _ _ (3 down) Effect. Gases help trap warmth to heat the Earth, but too many of these g _ _ _ _ (4 down) will create too much warmth. The gases that create the Greenhouse Effect include CO_2 or c _ _ _ _ _ _ d _ _ _ _ _ _ (1 down), chlorofluorocarbons or C _ _ _ (1 across) and m _ _ _ _ _ _ _ (7 across), a gas produced from swamps and by cattle. Too many CFCs damage the o _ _ _ _ (6 across) layer that protects our Earth. Natural gas, o _ _ (9 across) and c _ _ _ (5 across) are fossil fuels. They are burned to produce heat and e _ _ _ _ _ _ (10 across). This can also cause damage to plants by forming a _ _ _ r _ _ _ (8 down). Cars that use c _ _ _ _ _ _ _ _ _ (11 across) converters reduce air pollution which is called s _ _ _ (2 down).

World climatic regions and their problems

The world has many different climates – desert, tropical, equatorial, polar, mediterranean, coastal, continental and so on. Some big countries have several different climates in different areas. Each climatic region has its own problems that affect its environment.

♣ Below is a list of climatic regions. For each climate, choose from the two lists an example of a country where that climate occurs and a possible problem that can result.

Climatic region	Description	Country	Possible problem
Polar	Very cold, long winter and short cool summer.		
Continental	Very cold winters, hot summers.		
Coastal	Mild and wet, with four seasons.		
Mediterranean	Hot, dry summers, winter rain.		
Tropical	Wet and dry seasons.		
Equatorial	No seasons – humid, hot and wet all year.		
Desert	Very dry, little or no rain.		

Countries

Sudan

Spain

England

Australia

Russia

Antarctica

Brazil

Problems

• Rainforests being destroyed.

• Droughts destroy crops.

• Deserts spread.

• Mining companies destroy land.

• Tourism causes land pollution.

• Acid rain.

The world's rainfall

       The world's rainfall

Not all places in the world have enough rain for crops to grow. The graph opposite shows how much rain several places in the world receive each year.

❖ Use an atlas and the graph to answer the following questions:

• In which places might water shortages be a problem?
• Which places have the same amount of rain as London?
• In which country is Columbia?
• Which places are in the tropics?
• Which places have twice as much rainfall as London? In which countries are they located?

❖ Find all the places on the graph in your atlas.

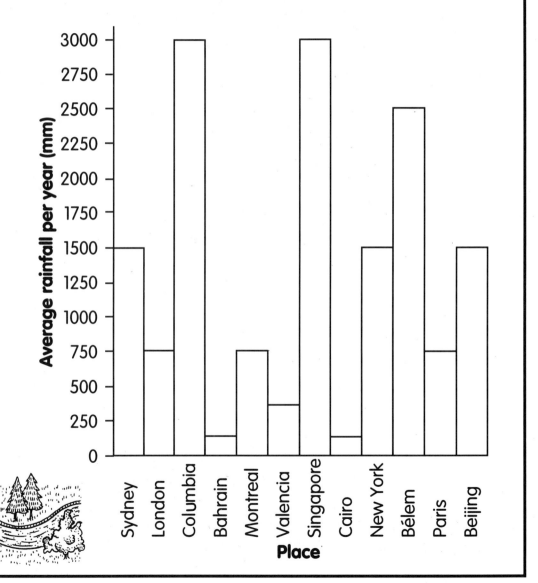

Alphabet dot-to-dot

♣ Complete these two pictures by joining up the letters of the alphabet in the correct order.

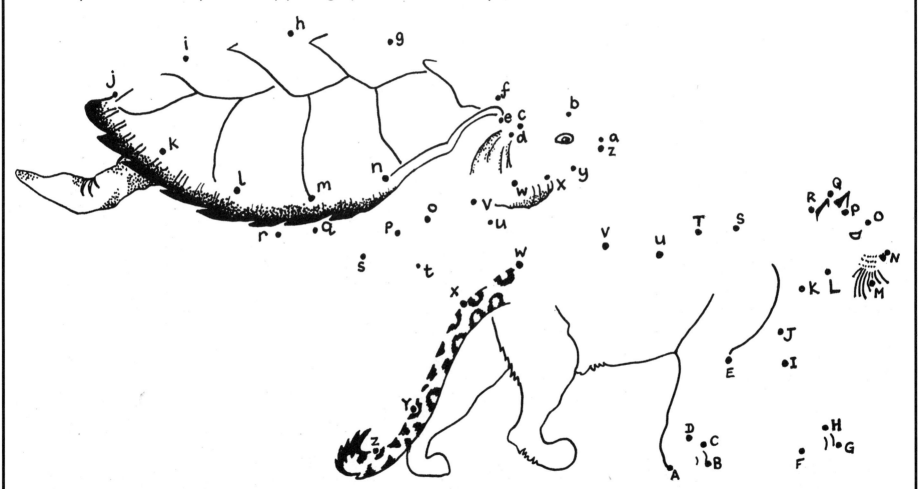

♣ Colour each picture. You will now have pictures of two endangered animals – what are they?
♣ Why are these animals endangered?

Name _____

Number dot-to-dot

❖ Work out each of the following problems.

1 3 + 2 =

2 2 + 2 =

3 5 + 1 =

4 5 + 5 =

5 4 + 3 =

6 6 + 3 =

7 2 + 0 =

8 2 + 1 =

9 0 + 1 =

10 4 + 4 =

❖ Join the **answer** to problem 1 to the **answer** to problem 2, the **answer** to problem 2 to the **answer** to problem 3 and so on.

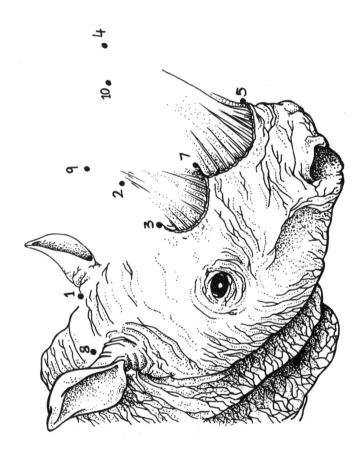

❖ What have you drawn?

❖ Why is this animal endangered?

Name _____

Endangered species jigsaw

✤ Cut out these jigsaw pieces.
✤ Join the pieces together. You will have a picture of some endangered animals.
✤ Find out what species are shown on this puzzle and why they are endangered.

Planning a wildlife area

Planning a wildlife area

Small Town Primary School is planning a wildlife area in the school grounds. Help them decide where everything should go.

♣ Cut out each item below and put it on the map in the best place.

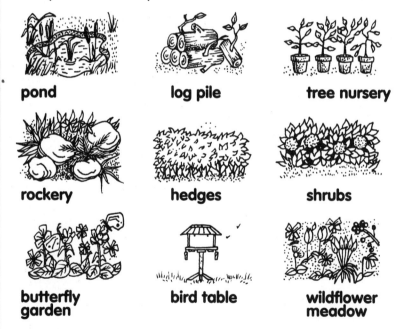

pond **log pile** **tree nursery**

rockery **hedges** **shrubs**

butterfly garden **bird table** **wildflower meadow**

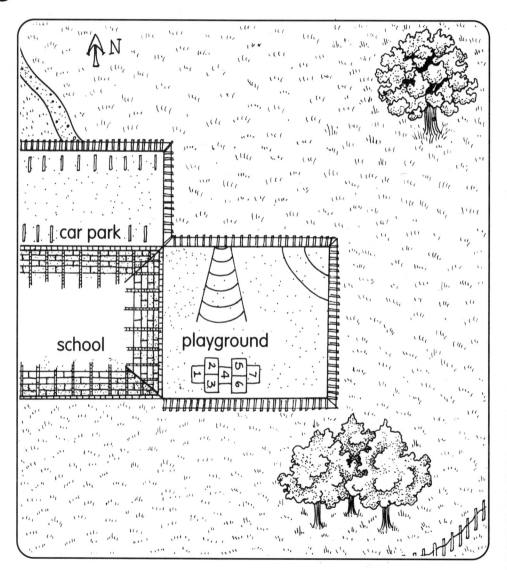

♣ Consider:
• Which items need to be in the sun?
• Which items need to be in the shade?
• Do any items need protection from the wind?

124

Name _____

Design a T-shirt

✤ Design a T-shirt to get the message across about one of these issues:
• Save our rainforests
• Protect rare animal species
• Plant a tree.

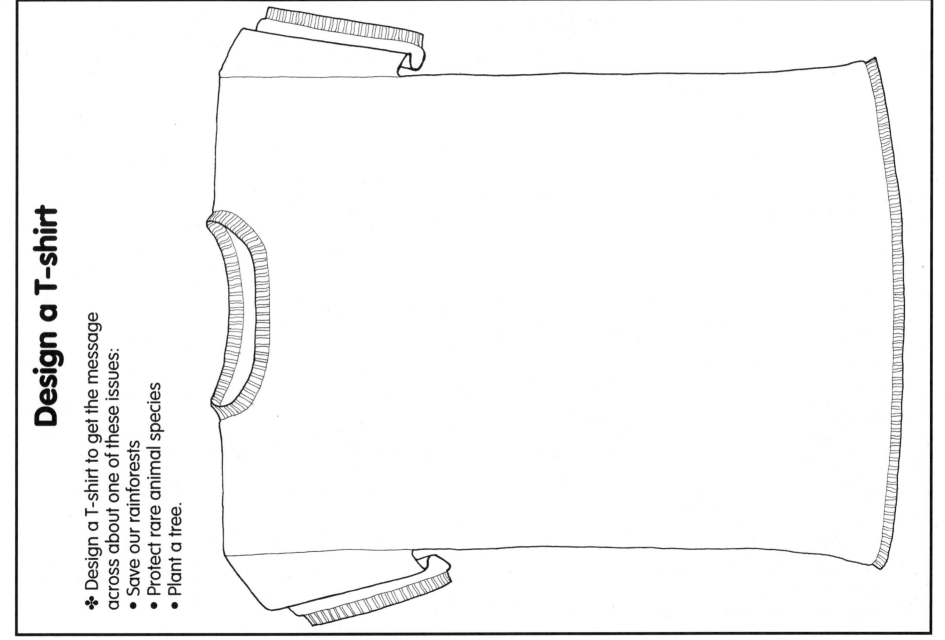

Caring for our wildlife

Name _____

Caring for our wildlife

✿ Find these words in the grid below.
Put a circle around each word as you find it.

habitat	species	wildlife	endangered
survival	protect	caring	natural
extinction	adaptation	respect	reserve
conservation	rare	flora	fauna

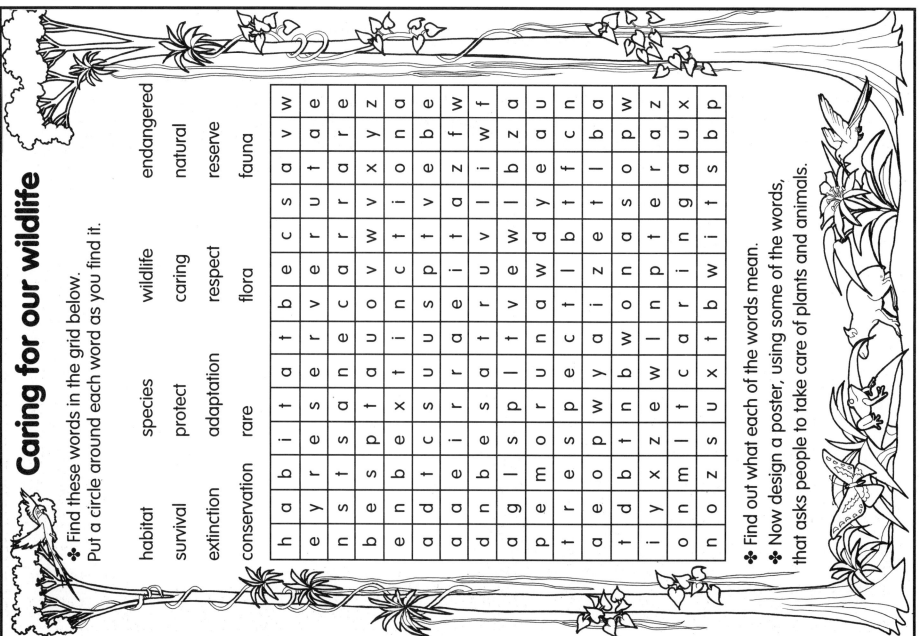

h	a	b	i	t	a	t	b	e	c	s	a	v	w
e	y	r	e	s	e	r	v	e	r	u	t	a	e
n	s	t	s	a	n	e	c	a	r	a	r	e	e
b	e	s	p	t	a	u	o	v	w	x	y	z	z
e	n	b	e	x	t	i	n	c	t	i	o	n	a
a	d	t	c	s	u	u	s	p	t	v	e	b	e
a	a	e	i	r	r	a	e	i	t	a	z	f	w
d	n	b	e	s	a	t	r	u	v	l	i	w	f
a	g	l	s	p	l	t	v	e	w	l	b	z	a
p	e	m	o	r	u	n	a	w	d	y	e	a	u
t	r	e	s	p	e	c	t	l	b	t	f	c	n
a	e	o	p	w	y	a	i	z	e	t	l	b	a
t	d	b	t	n	b	w	o	n	a	s	o	p	w
i	y	x	z	e	w	l	n	p	t	e	r	a	z
o	n	m	l	t	c	a	r	i	n	g	a	u	x
n	o	z	s	u	x	t	b	w	i	t	s	b	p

✿ Find out what each of the words mean.
✿ Now design a poster, using some of the words,
that asks people to take care of plants and animals.

Name _____

Protecting our wildlife

♣ Use the word bank below to help you to write about how and why we should protect the world's wildlife. Use reference books too.
♣ Display your writing for others to read.

protect	endangered
species	extinct
caring	conservation
saving	environment
danger	threatened
exist	preserve
problem	habitat
native	jewellery
rare	sanctuary
reserves	creature

'Saving our plants and animals' writing paper

Name _____

Saving our plants and animals

_____

_____

_____

_____

_____

_____

_____

_____

_____

_____

_____

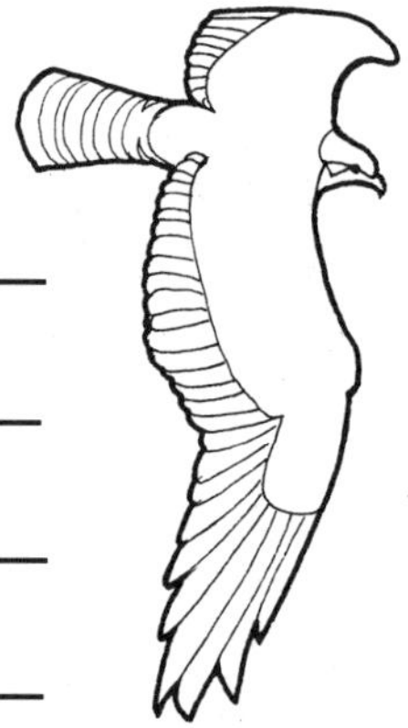

Extinct animals

Many animals no longer exist; they have become extinct.

❧ Match each of these pictures of extinct animals to the correct name in the list below.
❧ Add whether the creature was a mammal or bird. (The first one has been done for you.)
❧ Find out why these creatures became extinct.

moa
dodo
aurochs
quagga
pink-headed duck
passenger pigeon
steller's sea cow
great auk

Name: dodo
Type: bird

Name: _____
Type: _____

Name: _____
Type: _____

Name: _____
Type: _____

Name: _____
Type: _____

Name: _____
Type: _____

Name: _____
Type: _____

Name: _____
Type: _____

Name _____

Endangered animal species

The following animals are considered to be endangered: common dormouse, giant panda, tiger and osprey.

✤ Find out why they are endangered.

✤ Now find out more about them – where they live, how they live, what they eat and so on.

✤ For each animal, draw a picture of it in the first box and then write the information you have found out next to it.

	Information:
common dormouse	

	Information:
giant panda	

	Information:
tiger	

	Information:
osprey	

Animals at risk

All the animals below are considered to be 'at risk'.

✤ Find out why the numbers of these animals are falling.
✤ Suggest ways to help save these animals from becoming extinct.

Animal at risk	Reason why it is at risk	Possible solutions to save it
African elephant		
scarlet macaw		
black rhinoceros		
blue whale		

Threats to wildlife

Name _____

Threats to wildlife

All the things shown below threaten wildlife in some way.
♣ For each item, suggest which types of wildlife might be at risk and possible solutions
to the problems of each one.

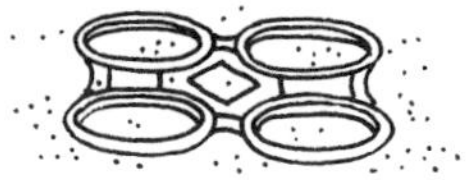

plastic can carriers

Wildlife at risk: _____
_____
_____

Solution: _____
_____
_____

oil spillages

Wildlife at risk: _____
_____
_____

Solution: _____
_____
_____

broken glass bottles

Wildlife at risk: _____
_____
_____

Solution: _____
_____
_____

empty drink cans

Wildlife at risk: _____
_____
_____

Solution: _____
_____
_____

old fishing tackle

Wildlife at risk: _____
_____
_____

Solution: _____
_____
_____

hedge clearing

Wildlife at risk: _____
_____
_____

Solution: _____
_____
_____

insecticides

Wildlife at risk: _____
_____
_____

Solution: _____
_____
_____

dumping waste

Wildlife at risk: _____
_____
_____

Solution: _____
_____
_____

Save for a good cause

Make this money box and use it to save for a good cause, for example a local animal sanctuary.

♣ Draw and colour designs on each square. Write your name on the base of the cube. (This square will not need to be coloured.)

A

Name:

_____

B

Tab A fits into slot B to keep the money box shut.

Cut out slot

Cut out slot B

♣ Think about your design and a message, such as: 'Save the sanctuary'.

♣ Cut out the box and glue it together using the tabs.

Animal alliteration

Animal alliteration

Alliteration is where most words in a phrase or sentence begin with the same letter. Here are several examples, to give you ideas:

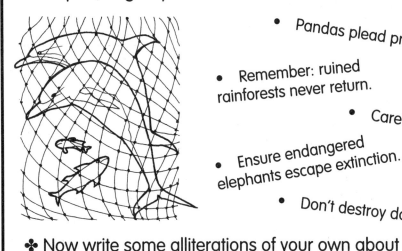

- Pandas plead protection.

- Remember: ruined rainforests never return.

- Care for crocs.

- Ensure endangered elephants escape extinction.

- Don't destroy dolphins.

♣ Now write some alliterations of your own about protecting plants and animals below.

_____

_____

_____

_____

♣ Design a poster in this space using one of your alliterations as the slogan.

What do plants need?

What do plants need?

♣ Carry out this experiment to find out what plants need to grow strong and healthy. You will need: bean seeds, potting soil, sand, water, six pots. Plant the bean seeds under the following conditions and record what happens.

Condition	Prediction – will the beans grow?	Observations			
		Week 1	Week 2	Week 3	Week 4
potting soil water sunlight					
potting soil water in the dark					
potting soil no water sunlight					
potting soil no water in the dark					
sand water sunlight					
water sunlight					

In the zoo

Name _____

In the zoo

Although zoos may not be ideal homes for animals, many zoos have saved animals from becoming extinct and, therefore, have a very important role to play in protecting endangered species.

♣ Can you find your way around this zoo? Following Marilyn's directions, draw her the route on the map to find out where Graham will meet her.

♣ When you have solved this problem, make up some directions for a friend to follow.

Dear Graham,
    Meet us for lunch at the zoo. Just follow these directions:
• From the main entrance, go north.
• Turn east at the first junction, then south, then east again.
• Go north and take the first turn on your right.
• At the junction, go south.
    We'll meet you there.
                    Marilyn

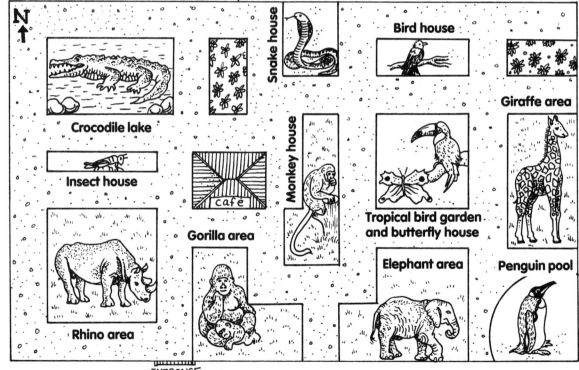

♣ Which of the animals in this zoo are endangered in the wild? List them on the back of the sheet.

What do you think?

✤ Read the following statements.

✤ Write down whether you agree or disagree with each statement and then write down what **you** think about each one.

✤ Share your opinions with others.

Statements	Do you agree or disagree?	Your opinion
It's OK to keep endangered species as pets; at least they will be safe.		
Zoos are good places for animals to live.		
We should allow poor countries to cut down rainforests; they need money from farming.		
Humans are more important than animals. We need to think about ourselves first.		

Our effect on wildlife

Name _____

Our effect on wildlife

All the answers to the puzzle below are the names of endangered animal species.
The clues tell you why they have become threatened.
♣ Complete the puzzle.
♣ Find out how we can protect these animals.

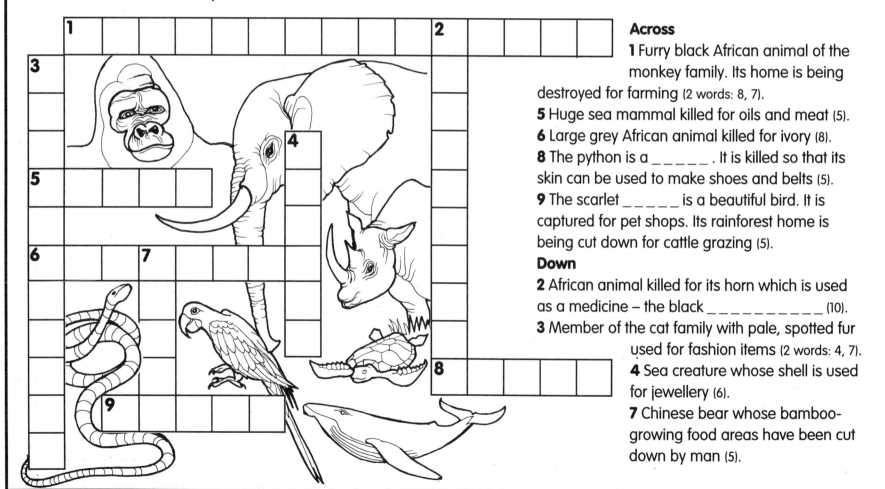

Across
1 Furry black African animal of the monkey family. Its home is being destroyed for farming (2 words: 8, 7).
5 Huge sea mammal killed for oils and meat (5).
6 Large grey African animal killed for ivory (8).
8 The python is a _ _ _ _ _ . It is killed so that its skin can be used to make shoes and belts (5).
9 The scarlet _ _ _ _ _ is a beautiful bird. It is captured for pet shops. Its rainforest home is being cut down for cattle grazing (5).

Down
2 African animal killed for its horn which is used as a medicine – the black _ _ _ _ _ _ _ _ _ _ (10).
3 Member of the cat family with pale, spotted fur used for fashion items (2 words: 4, 7).
4 Sea creature whose shell is used for jewellery (6).
7 Chinese bear whose bamboo-growing food areas have been cut down by man (5).

Name _____

Detecting pollution

Lichens are the result of two types of plant, an alga and a fungus, living in partnership. Lichens can show how polluted the air is – they are pollution indicators. Lichens are damaged by acid, so the kind of pollution that causes acid rain determines the types of lichen that can grow.

♣ Conduct this survey covering as wide an area as possible, such as a whole town. Look at the lichens growing on the tombstones in the cemetries – a good place for them to grow.

Pollution indicator	
Type of lichen	Level of pollution
no lichen	very polluted air
crusty lichen	polluted air
leafy lichen	slightly polluted air
shrubby lichen	little pollution

Cemetry location	Type of lichen found	Level of pollution
Middle of town – heavy traffic		
Near a smoky factory		
Edge of town – where there are houses and some traffic		
In the countryside – little traffic, no factories and no farm spraying		
Other		

Endangered species around the world

Endangered species around the world

Animals all over the world are becoming endangered.

❧ Find out where the animals listed below live.
❧ Using the key provided, mark the place where each animal lives on the map opposite.

Key

p	giant panda
m	mountain gorilla
e	African elephant
r	black rhinoceros
b	bald eagle
w	wombat
d	common dormouse
rb	rabbit-bandicoot
j	jaguar
sl	snow leopard
t	tiger
sm	scarlet macaw
y	yak

Fact or opinion?

♣ Read the statements below. Decide if each statement is a fact or an opinion.

♣ Group the statements into facts and opinions.

♣ Share your choices with others. Do you all agree? Can a whole class agreement be achieved? Give reasons for your choices.

Horrible creatures such as poisonous spiders and crocodiles don't need to be protected.

Plants in the rainforest provide valuable medicines.

Hunting and fishing should be banned.

Some animals in the wild need to be killed every year to keep down their numbers.

People shouldn't eat meat.

One species of plant or animal becomes extinct every year.

Using animals to test new medicines helps saves lives.

All animals, including us, depend on plants to live.

If we cut down the forests, they will soon grow back.

Clothing and jewellery made from animals are more beautiful than synthetic articles.

All sharks should be killed because they can kill people.

No tree should ever be cut down.

Food chains

Name _____

Food chains

Plants are able to make their own food by photosynthesis, using energy from the sun, carbon dioxide, chlorophyll and water. Animals do not make their own food; they need to eat other animals or plants. These animals in turn may be eaten by other animals and so on. This is called a food chain. If the environment becomes polluted in some way, poisons can be passed along the food chain, causing the animal at the top or end of the chain to become ill.

♣ Look at the food chains given opposite. For each chain, choose a possible source of pollution from the list of suggestions below.

Possible sources of pollution
- acid rain
- chemical sprays from farms
- poisonous substances on landfill sites
- sewage dumped at sea
- garden slug pellets

Remember: Humans are often at the end of a food chain and, therefore, these pollutants can harm us too!

- leaf   caterpillar   mouse   owl

possible source of pollution to leaf: _____

- algae   small fish   bigger fish   human

possible source of pollution to small fish: _____

- leaf   slug   hedgehog

possible source of pollution to leaf: _____

- scraps   beetle   shrew   fox

possible source of pollution to scraps: _____

Tropical rainforests

The initial letters on the map below show where rainforests occur.
♣ Using an atlas, name these countries and list them on the back of this sheet.
(There are 22.)

♣ Why are the rainforests being destroyed?
♣ Suggest ways in which we can save the rainforests.

Countries where rainforests occur.

Conservation projects

Name _____

Conservation projects

Many natural environments around the world need extra care and protection. Most countries have set aside special areas called national parks or wildlife reserves where plants and animals can be protected. The world's first national park was founded in 1872 at Yellowstone in the USA.

♣ Use an atlas to find the countries in which these reserves are located.

Yellowstone	Coto Donana
Snowdonia	Masai Mara
Serengeti	Kushiro
Manu	Yankari
Amazonia	Jasper/Banff
Ayers Rock	Kanha
Pilanesberg	PoyangHu
North-east Greenland	Taimyr

♣ Mark them on this map by colouring them in green.

♣ Why do you think that it is important to protect certain environments? Share your ideas with others.